Stop Speaking for Free!

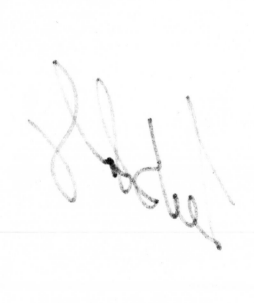

Speakers Are Raving About "Stop Speaking for Free!"

"I wouldn't think of doing a webinar without the advice and guidance in *Stop Speaking for Free!* by Lee Salz. He knows it all."
- Anne Miller, author of *Metaphorically Selling*

"Lee Salz, the King of Webinar Success, has written a book no one else could write. His webinar firm has made it possible for many of us to amplify our fame as business experts and deliver our expertise in a convenient, effective format. No one knows more about this topic than Lee, nor has better demonstrated its tenets in real life."
- Ken Lizotte, author of *The Expert's Edge*

"Lee Salz has taken the most pragmatic approach to webinars that I have seen in the web conferencing industry. He doesn't just talk about abstract tips and best practices, he demands that webinars serve a revenue-generating business need, and he helps companies meet that goal. Lee's creation of online infrastructure, documentation, and support services for business webinars is unique. Anybody looking to make money from webinars should take heed of his advice."
- Ken Molay, President of Webinar Success

"I spend a great deal of time on the road with my Blitz Experience training business. Attendee-funded webinars offer a terrific supplemental income stream for my business whether I'm in the office or traveling. The teachings in *Stop Speaking for Free!* help you understand what it takes to succeed when using webinars to generate income. A must-read for any business speaker, trainer, or consultant!"
- Andrea Sittig-Rolf, author of *Power Referrals*

Speakers Are Raving About "Stop Speaking for Free!"

"Stop Speaking for Free! provides great practical advice on effective techniques for planning, marketing, and delivering attendee-funded virtual training programs. From personal experience, I've learned these ideas really work – every speaker, author, trainer, and consultant will learn to increase revenue and drive new business."

- Gary Gack, owner of Process-Fusion.net

"I had the expertise in my subject matter, but this book helped me take that expertise and produce attendee-funded webinars easily and cheaply for my clients. The tips given are concrete, simple – and bottom-line, they work!"

- Susan Hoekstra, customer service expert and author of *The Service Journey*

"If you are a speaker, trainer or consultant, *Stop Speaking for Free!* is for you! Webinars are one of the strongest ways to reach an audience, demonstrate your expertise and drive new business. Lee Salz has helped more people build a webinar business than anyone else on the planet."

- Andy Miller, sales strategist to fast growth CEO's

"Lee Salz knows his stuff! From A to Z, Lee shares his expertise and knowledge on everything to help you conduct a successful attendee-funded webinar. Areas such as: selecting the most saleable content, designing the presentation, and using LinkedIn® to promote your webinar are just some of the highlights of this book. This is the place to start if you are even thinking about delivering your own attendee-funded webinar!"

- Teri Yanovitch, President of T.A. Yanovitch Inc.

Speakers Are Raving About "Stop Speaking for Free!"

"The high cost of travel, the threats of terrorism and the concern about disease have all put a damper on corporations' appetite for traveling freely. The days of hopping on an airplane to attend a seminar are quickly coming to an end. Business people are demanding training that is timely, relevant and accessible. The secrets found in *Stop Speaking for Free!* eliminate years of trial and error. This book is a must-have addition to any business library!"

- Barry Siskind, author of *Powerful Exhibit Marketing* and *Selling From the Inside Out*

"Lee Salz has mastered the art of the 'win-win webinar.' He has developed a systematic approach that brings value to both the participant and the speaker. He makes it look easy, but there's a true science behind his methods. This book will equip you with the skills to create a powerful and profitable program without having to reinvent the webinar wheel."

- Sandra Sellani, brand consultant and author of *What's Your BQ™* (Brand Quotient)

"Being an expert is one thing, but making money at it is a very different skill altogether. Lee Salz is the best at helping the 'everyday expert' learn how to brand their expertise and harvest the money that's out there using webinars. Lee is the one I go to for the right advice, and I highly recommend *Stop Speaking for Free!.*"

- Bill Guertin, author of *Reality Sells* and *The 800 Pound Gorilla of Sales*

"Lee is the king of attendee-funded webinars. He knows exactly how to help you make money in this crazy economic world we live in. Lee is way ahead of the curve."

- Dr. Julie Miller, author of *Business Writing That Counts*

Speakers Are Raving About "Stop Speaking for Free!"

"Nobody knows promoting business with webinars like Lee Salz, and his new book, *Stop Speaking for Free!*, should be on every entrepreneur's bookshelf. While this unique guide is packed with insider information on successful webinar marketing, the chapter entitled *Getting Media Attention for Your Virtual Training Events – Promote Your Attendee-Funded Webinars for Pennies* is alone worth the price of admission."

- Danita Bye, CEO and founder of Sales Growth Specialists

"Lee Salz is the master of the attendee-funded webinar. His skills and knowledge combined with his innate marketing ability have made him a valuable resource for speakers and audiences alike."

- Peg Jackson, Principal of Adjunct LLC, and author of *Reputational Risk Managment* and *Sarbanes-Oxley for Small Business*

"I have implemented several of Lee's strategies to drive attendance to my attendee-funded webinars and found all of them beneficial. Webinars are a measurable (and cost-efficient) learning tool for business people to acquire the skills they need to succeed."

- Janet Boulter, Center Consulting Group

"Lee Salz is a Black Belt Master at promotion and sales, and he's designed the premier platform for monetizing webinars. In *Stop Speaking for Free!*, Lee reveals the trade secrets he's developed as a pioneer in delivering business training content on the web and doing it profitably. Lee and his team are hands-down the best in their field. Lee's book must be within arm's length as you prepare, market and deliver your webinar!"

- Jim Bouchard, speaker, Black Belt Mindset Master and author of *Think Like a Black Belt*

Speakers Are Raving About "Stop Speaking for Free!"

"The help I received in preparing my PowerPoint slides, especially adding the graphics, was invaluable. I thought I knew how to put together slides, and I learned quite a number of helpful tips. Thank you."

- Barbara Pachter, business etiquette speaker and author of *New Rules @ Work*

"Having multiple streams of income and leads is always worthwhile. *Stop Speaking for Free!* provides the 'how' that when applied will simply, effectively and consistently make money - as much or as little as you desire."

- Dr. Richard Norris MBA, Head of Global Development, Lifestyle Architecture

"Working with Lee's company, Business Expert Webinars, has been an eye opener. One could think that delivering a profitable webinar is simple and anyone can do it effectively; in reality; it takes special understanding and talent to pull off an effective, well-attended webinar. Lee has gone down all the roads to find out what works and what wastes your time. Before you spend a great deal of your time, effort and frustration, take in the depth of input and insight provided in *Stop Speaking for Free!* It will save you time, dollars and get you on the right track to successful webinars that provide you a return! "

- Harlan Goerger, President, H. Goerger & Associates, author of *The Selling Gap: Selling Strategies for the 21st Century*

"In working with Lee Salz and his team, I have learned in one resource how to take my webinars and presentations in general to the next level. The resources they provided in the area of attendee-funded webinar marketing to drive registration were especially helpful. My new skills have enabled me to create new ways to help my clients. As a business owner, that is invaluable."

- Colette M. Releford, President, Strive Business Solutions

Speakers Are Raving About "Stop Speaking for Free!"

"If you are ready to grow your training and consulting business by offering attendee-funded webinars, then read and re-read this brilliant book by my friend, Lee Salz. It is a brilliant step-by-step guide to filling your valuable events with paid enrollments!"

- Dianne Crampton, author of *TIGERS Among Us* and *Team WaHOO*

"Webinars can provide an excellent format for educational content about your products and services. You can also generate a significant revenue stream from them. *Stop Speaking for Free!* contains all the information you will ever need to produce successful webinars. A must read for anyone considering offering attendee-funded webinars."

- Garrett Colbert, Director of Sales, ConferTel

"Lee knows how to put together a webinar product people pay to attend to consistently play at the top of their game."

- Raj Gavurla, entrepreneurial speaker, author of *Winning at Entrepreneurship*

"Lee Salz has rapidly become the go-to resource in the area of attendee-funded webinars. Lee's expertise is indispensable and second to none. *Stop Speaking for Free!* walks you through the exact steps and teaches you how to monetize your expertise."

- Scott Barclay, President of Learning LLC

"Offering attendee-funded webinars is a great way to grow your consulting practice. It gives you a method to introduce your skill in a way that doesn't just 'hard sell' but provides true value to the attendees. *Stop Speaking for Free!* sets out a simple, proven strategy to help you establish your attendee-funded webinar model. It's the roadmap for anyone looking for a high-value way to reach prospects."

- Sarah Day, Small Business Growth Strategist

Speakers Are Raving About "Stop Speaking for Free!"

"Attendee-funded webinars open up a whole new revenue stream to you without leaving your office. Using content already created for in-person seminars, you can quickly create and deliver webinars that appeal to specific audiences anywhere in the world. Webinars expand your reach, expand your brand, and establish you as an expert in your field."

- Kirk Wilkinson, speaker, coach, and author of *The Happiness Factor*

"Lee Salz is way ahead of the curve when it comes to attendee-funded webinars. His formula for webinar success is unbeatable! He knows how to blend excellent content from qualified experts with targeted promotions that drives attendance."

- Lorraine Howell, author of *Give Your Elevator Speech a Lift!*

"If you intend to take your webinar revenue stream to the next level, this is your book. No smoke – just straight talk about what really works."

- Terry Slattery, Slattery Sales

"Lee Salz and his team at Business Expert Webinars provide in-depth training on how to develop quality webinar presentations. The team developed its knowledge through hands-on experience in the webinar business. This book will short-cut your learning curve."

- Denise Harrison, Vice President of the Center for Simplified Strategic Planning, Inc.

"Stop Speaking for Free! is so rich in content that you can't help but succeed at producing and delivering attendee-funded webinars! Not a detail is missing – you'll go deeper into the webinar reservoir than you ever thought possible."

- Patty Kreamer, CPO®, Certified Professional Organizer®

"Lee is a thought leader in the development of educational webinars. Lee's ability to focus on the big picture, listen and ask thoughtful questions provides great confidence for speakers. *Stop Speaking for Free!* delivers a practical, straightforward process that positions speakers for success."

- Hillary Feder, President of Ask Hillarys

"A diversified income stream for speakers is a necessity that helps overcome a slowdown in speaking engagements. The extra income stream, not only brings in money, but also provides a platform to demonstrate your expertise to a world-wide audience without ever leaving your office chair. *Stop Speaking for Free!* provides a detailed 'how to' for anyone who wants to enter the attendee-funded webinar space. Don't leave money on the table."

- Billy Arcement, ME.d, The Leadership Strategist

"One of the greatest assets for any business is having a support structure to help push your business success. The information in *Stop Speaking for Free!* is your immediate support team. The available resources not only tell you, but also illustrate for you, the necessary techniques to help you build income with attendee-funded webinars - the new genre in training and development. The information is practical, motivational and actionable. Read this now!"

- Drew Stevens, Ph.D., President of Drew Stevens Consulting

Stop Speaking for Free!

The Ultimate Guide to
Making Money With Webinars

Lee B. Salz

with Jenny L. Hamby

Business Expert Publishing
Thomson, Georgia

Business Expert Publishing
The Business Expert Publisher™
P.O. Box 1389
Thomson, GA 30824

Published by Business Expert Publishing
Printed in the United States of America

Cover Design: Dave Blaker

First Edition

ISBN-13: 978-1-935602-03-3
ISBN-10: 1935602039

Dedications

To my wife, Sharon, the love of my life, who is not only my soul-mate, but the key to my life's success.

To my children, Jamie, Steven, and David ... It is said that the role of a parent is to inspire their children to tackle challenges and help them grow. Yet, you inspire me every day to reach deep within to make myself a better person than yesterday. Never lose your passion to be the best you can be.

To my parents, Myra and Joseph Salz, thank you for instilling in me the importance of education and inspiring me to pursue my dreams.

To my sister, Marlo Salz, thank you for your support of my life's ventures.

An additional special thank you to Mom and Sharon for taking the time to edit this book.

To Jenny Hamby for her incredible support and dedication, not only with this book, but with Business Expert Webinars. I sincerely thank you for everything you have done for me and our speaker community.

To the Business Expert Webinars speakers, thank you for entrusting me with your journey to succeed with attendee-funded webinars.

Table of Contents

Table of Contents

Foreword

- If you ask 100 people, "Are webinars free?" most of them will answer, "Yes!"

- If you ask those same 100 people, "Is training free?" they will reply, "No!"

- Then ask the $64,000 question: "What about training webinars?"

Author, speaker, and sales management strategist, Lee Salz, believes the answer to that question is a no-brainer: Attendees will pay for training webinars. After all, speakers are providing more than just information in such webinars—they are furnishing training for which they would be paid had it been done in person. Salz isn't just presenting theory. He is the founder and CEO of Business Expert Webinars, which has grown a speaker portfolio of 150 strong with more than 750 webinars on its schedule ... every one of which is delivered as an attendee-funded virtual training event.

If you are a speaker, trainer, or consultant, figuring out how to offer attendee-funded webinars (AFWs) is not a luxury. It is a critical step you MUST take RIGHT NOW or risk the loss of your business and livelihood. *Why do I say that?*

Let's examine some training realities, starting with the economy—even though most of us would rather not talk about that these days. Costs are up, profits are down, and traveling for classroom-based training is a big no-no.

In fact, *Training* magazine's 2009 Industry Report found that the average spending per learner fell four percent to $1,036 from 2008 to 2009. Overall, the amount of total U.S. training industry spending — including payroll and spending on external products and services — declined seven percent from $56.2 billion in 2008 to $52.2 billion in 2009. Training payroll expenditures shed nearly $1 billion to $32.9 billion as companies reduced training headcount. Not surprisingly, some 47% of the nearly 1,000 study respondents indicated their training budget decreased over the last year.

During a recent webinar, we asked participants if their organizations were planning to further cut their training budgets. The good news is that 42% said no, indicating they recognize the competitive advantage of having well-trained employees. But in some cases, there is just no way around the financial realities, as indicated by the other 58% saying they were planning to cut their training budgets.

Another training reality is the fact that companies continue to expand globally, with offices around the world, and many companies now offer employees a telecommuting option, which has allowed them to reduce costs by closing physical offices. They are demanding more work from fewer employees, which means the amount of time for education is very limited. In addition, there is an influx of Millennial employees who are very comfortable with technology and prefer to learn hands-on via computer.

In fact, in an Everything DiSC® Workplace Survey of 4,384 training participants nationwide by Inscape Publishing, Inc., the following results were found:

- 94% of respondents agreed computer-based training was convenient for them.
- 43% said they did this computer-based training outside of their normal work hours.
- 90% said the computer-based format of the training was a big time saver for them.
- 76% said the training made them more effective at their job.
- 88% said they remember what they learned in the training.

These training realities mean many organizations are looking for alternatives to physical classroom training, which, although popular with many employees, does have its drawbacks. That's where training webinars come in. They offer employees the 1-2 punch of hands-on interactivity AND instructor-led training. And they offer employers the 1-2 punch of no investment in hardware and software AND quick, easy set-up and update functionality. Plus, employees don't need to go anywhere to participate in the training, which means no travel costs or lost travel time.

Training magazine's 2009 Industry Report found that 28.5% of training hours are delivered via webcast or computer-based methods, and 23% is delivered via blended learning methods. And 71% of the nearly 1,000 respondents use virtual classroom/webcasting/video broadcasting for training purposes. I expect those numbers to continue to climb, especially as the 73.5 million tech-savvy Gen-Yers continue to flood the workforce.

The first big hurdle for you to overcome is the perception that webinars are always free. They're not! More and more, there is recognition among trainers, speakers, and consultants that they need to be able to monetize their expertise by offering AFWs. And they are doing it. Remember, there was a time not long ago where everyone watched free TV. That's not the case today. People used to listen to the radio for free. Today, millions of people pay for satellite radio. Tap water once was good enough for everyone, but today people buy bottled water in droves. What these have in common is that there is perceived value in what is being purchased.

How does that relate to AFWs? The key is creating new, exclusive, skill-based training delivered via webinars and marketing it in a way that makes people say, "Wow! I really want to learn about this subject from this expert (and I don't mind paying for the opportunity to do so)."

This book offers a soup-to-nuts guide for doing just that. The rest is up to you. But don't wait too long — opportunity often doesn't knock twice.

Lorri Freifeld, Editor-in-Chief,
Training and *Sales & Marketing Management* magazines

Introduction

A few years ago, I was asked to deliver a webinar for an association on how to identify and hire the right sales people. The webinar was free to participants, but a sponsor paid $25,000 to be part of the event. More than 1,400 people attended the webinar, and my compensation as the speaker was exposure. Ever try to pay your mortgage with exposure? It's certainly not the most useful currency.

This experience got me thinking. If more than 1,400 people saw value in my content such that they would invest an hour of their time with me, there must be others who would invest money to access my training content. I decided to formulate a program that would allow me to deliver my sales management training through webinars for which attendees would pay to attend. I knew that charging a fee would scare many prospects away, but I realized that even if I got five percent of the turnout as the free event, I could make real money by delivering attendee-funded webinars (AFWs).

As a speaker, I was a solopreneur, which meant that time was my enemy. There are always tons of great ideas out there, but not necessarily adequate time to pursue all of them. As much as I loved the idea of implementing AFWs into my speaking business, I didn't have the time to invest to actively market them beyond my own database list or operationalize them. I also recognized that I needed expert help ... someone to review my presentation, consult with me on marketing, etc. I went looking for a firm that had a marketing reach bigger than my own and would deal with the operational mechanics, such as registration, credit card processing, event management, and other tasks. I was shocked when my Google searches found nothing!

I am wired in such a way that when I find a business gap, I develop a model to bridge it. Surely, I could not be the only speaker who had stumbled onto the opportunity presented by AFWs, yet was too time-challenged to properly add the offering to their business. Thus, I naively launched Business Expert Webinars (BEW), which today is a leading provider of business eLearning training.

Why did I say naively? Armed with 20/20 hindsight, most entrepreneurs can look back to the launch of their businesses and recognize they didn't know as much as they thought they did at the time. The successful ones go in with their eyes wide open, fully expecting to get an education along the way and are prepared to adapt their business. My naïveté came to light during my interaction with the speakers whom I interviewed to participate in the BEW eLearning program. We had great conversations. Speakers would describe fantastic virtual training events that would be tremendously valuable to the attendees. I would wrap up the conversations with "This sounds great! Go ahead and email the program description to me, and we'll put the event on our website."

Then, it happened. The speaker emailed the webinar description to me – a description that typically consisted of a sentence and two bullet points. Knowing that no one would pay for online training with such a limited description, I sent an email to the speaker advising them that the description needed more meat. Unfortunately, I discovered that speakers are speakers for a reason – although they could effectively share their wisdom, they were at a loss about how to develop a compelling webinar description that would put attendees in virtual seats.

I quickly realized that I had a business-limiting problem. Copywriting was not my core competency. I had enjoyed a 20+ year career building sales and marketing organizations, but selling through print was a different ballgame. Although I was not a professional copywriter, I came to the realization that the webinar description was the product, and our product was awful. I read the descriptions for the webinars we had for sale on BEW and was dismayed. I knew there was no way I would pay for these events based on what was presented as the product. There was a huge disconnect. What the speakers were teaching was stellar, but the product representation was inadequate.

I began to research the subject of webinar and teleseminar marketing and found that what was written was focused on driving attendance in free events, not attendee-funded ones. At first, this frustrated me. I didn't realize that these were uncharted waters, but they were. The primary use of webinars had been for marketing purposes – to build mailing lists or sell products and services. Nothing had been written about how to successfully offer webinars for which attendees would pay to participate.

Not to condemn the free webinar market, but it is not difficult to convert prospects to registrants when you are offering a free event. Authors who write about how to promote free webinars focus on what is commonly called "marketing reach," also known as "getting the word out." The description of a free webinar is usually brief and often starts with, "In this webinar, you will learn...." However, the scrutiny with which prospects review a free webinar invitation is not complex. If they are the slightest bit interested, they sign up. But you're incredibly lucky if you can get even 25% of the registrants to show up.

Convincing people to spend money to attend a webinar is different. I was asking prospects to make an investment in themselves or their employees to attend a virtual training event. I wasn't asking for the king's ransom to participate in the webinar, but it still meant entering the digits of a credit card as opposed to just clicking a button to join for free.

In addition to recognizing that AFWs required more work to convert prospects to registrations, I noticed that the general public had developed a jaded-eye about webinars. Because the main thrust of the free webinar space is for marketing or sales as opposed to delivering a pure training session, a bait-and-switch feeling had grown among webinar participants. Too often, they signed up to learn something, but soon discovered that they were attending a 60-minute infomercial. As a matter of fact, soon after launching BEW, I signed up for a free webinar about delivering your educational content online, a very relevant event considering where my attention was focused. I left the event after 25 minutes, angry and frustrated that I had forgotten what the free webinar market was all about. I had learned nothing about online education, but had been taken on a mind-numbing tour of the features and functions of a vendor's webinar technology.

All of this meant that I was back to square one. I recognized that BEW needed a methodology to write webinar descriptions designed for the attendee-funded marketplace. I was not a copywriter by trade, but I knew sales. I had written an award-winning book on sales strategy and tactics published by WBusinessBooks a few years earlier. I recognized that sales concepts needed to be used when writing webinar descriptions. Successful sales people do not start meetings with prospects by opening their briefcases and preaching about their products. Doing so would guarantee that they would not make the sale. The same holds true when writing descriptions for AFWs. Starting a webinar description with "in this webinar, you will learn" was the copywriting equivalent of the aforementioned sales faux pas. No sale for the sales person, and no signups for the webinar.

I'm not overly spiritual and generally not a believer in fate, but that's the only way I can describe finding Jenny Hamby. Jenny had been interviewed on a website that also publishes my articles. She had put together an incredible home-study course, "How to Successfully Market Seminars and Workshops." I listened to the interview in which she talked about what it took to get attendees into seminars and was blown away. I immediately sent her an email saying, "We need to talk!" After looking at the webinar descriptions on my site, she diplomatically concurred that there was room for improvement, as well as with my assessment of how AFWs needed to be marketed.

That's when things got interesting. Jenny believed that many of the principles that were used to generate paid registrations for in-person seminars could be applied to the AFW marketplace. While the buying process was different, many of her techniques could be applied to generate registrations for webinars.

We spent countless hours reviewing BEW data and formulated a specialized copywriting methodology for webinar descriptions geared specifically to attendee-funded webinars and a promotional strategy that aligned with the unique buying process for AFWs.

The results of our collaboration were staggering. Registrant conversions on BEW skyrocketed, with some webinars selling four times greater than standard Internet conversion rates.

In this book, we share the BEW formula for attendee-funded webinar success with speakers, trainers, coaches and consultants who recognize the opportunity presented by AFWs, so they can incorporate it into their overall business strategy. Inside, you'll discover a comprehensive, step-by-step process to help you succeed with AFWs, from picking your topic, to writing the description, to promoting the virtual training event. It is my hope that you will use the tools presented in this book to turn webinars into a steady revenue stream for *your* business.

Lee B. Salz, Founder and Chief Executive Officer,
Business Expert Webinars

1 | Analyzing the Attendee-Funded Webinar Opportunity

Why For-Fee Virtual Events Belong In Your Product Portfolio

In the last few years, the growth of eLearning has been booming. Even as the economy circles in uncertainty, companies and professionals alike are flocking to virtual learning opportunities as a way to continue their professional development.

Many factors are driving this trend. First and foremost, we are busier than ever as a society. Your prospects and clientele are under ever-increasing pressure to get more done in less time. And webinars offer the ultimate experience for people seeking training in a convenient format. Not only is it possible to participate in virtual events without leaving your home or office, participants can sign up at the last minute – literally. They can attend in their pajamas if they want. And if you offer on-demand training, they can even participate when and where it best fits their schedules.

In addition, eLearning delivers education in bite-sized chunks, which is appealing to people with little time. Even if it is possible to find time to attend a two-day workshop, the idea of immersing yourself in two days worth of content can be overwhelming for some people. These individuals will refuse to attend a daylong or multi-day training program merely because they know that they won't have the time or energy to absorb all of the teachings, much less implement them.

By contrast, the shorter format of a webinar allows busy people to easily incorporate education and skill development into an already packed schedule. For example, it might take several days to teach a business owner everything he needs to know and do to properly optimize his web site for search engine traffic. However, in an hour, you could teach him how to select the right keywords that will boost the site's search engine ranking.

Webinars are also growing in popularity because they are cost-effective modes of training. Most companies and individuals are working with tighter budgets. And when budgets are cut, training is one of the first line items to be trimmed. Virtual training provides much-needed training in a format – and with a price tag – that fits most organizations' smaller budgets by saving on tuition and travel expenses. In addition to eliminating the need for costly travel, webinar tuition is economical when compared to seminars. Spending several hundred dollars on a seminar might seem extravagant and risky to some managers, whereas spending $75 to $400 on a webinar appears reasonable and more affordable. The fact that the per-hour fee may be higher with virtual training than in-person training becomes irrelevant: no travel required, a smaller total price tag, and the promise of skill improvement.

Is Fear Holding You Back?

Some speakers, consultants and experts have resisted the idea of adding webinars to their portfolio of products because they are fearful of webinar technology. Others refuse to make the shift because they don't know how to translate the content they normally deliver through in-person training events to a virtual platform.

If you're reading this book, chances are good that you are ready to embrace the technology that will enable you to deliver a vibrant, virtual learning experience for your clients. But if you are still resisting the shift to this robust teaching platform and using the excuse that you can deliver your material just as well in the form of a teleseminar, my advice is simple: **Get over it!** If you want clients to regard you as cutting-edge and to deliver a higher-impact training program, it's essential to become comfortable working with webinar technology. Teleseminars limit your interaction with clients to the auditory realm only and make it more difficult to engage the visual learner. It's also "yesterday's technology" as far as training is concerned.

Overcoming the technology barrier is as simple as familiarizing yourself with the technology you're using. Most webinar providers offer recorded tutorials or one-on-one training programs to ensure that presenters are completely comfortable with the platform used to deliver webinars. Many also provide you with a free "demo account" so you can practice your webinar before you deliver it.

Why Attendee-Funded Webinars (AFWs) Belong in Your Product Portfolio

There are several reasons to incorporate AFWs into your portfolio of offerings:

Add streams of revenue. The recent economic downturn exposed a dangerous weakness in many speakers' businesses: relying too much on traditional speaking engagements. When training budgets were cut, as they typically are when corporate executives issue instructions to start trimming expenses, speakers saw their bookings drop. Without revenue from other sources, many talented professionals found themselves in dire financial straits. AFWs are an easy way to diversify your offerings, so that when one stream of income is adversely affected by factors outside of your control, you still have an option for bringing in much-needed revenue.

Increase revenue and profits. By offering virtual training that appeals to different segments or a wider segment of your audience, you will increase your revenue. If you offer only in-person training workshops, for example, only a certain segment of your audience will participate. By adding webinars to your repertoire, you provide an offering that appeals to people who don't have the budget to attend an in-person workshop. This additional training option allows you to capture more clients and sales.

AFWs also allow you to turn more of your days into revenue-producing days. Increasing your revenue can be as simple as filling in holes in your speaking schedule with AFWs. Because they are relatively inexpensive to produce, the revenue you generate will be mostly profit.

Are you currently offering attendee-funded teleseminars? Offering webinars instead may allow you to increase your revenue, as well. The enhanced learning environment you are able to create in a webinar may enable you to justify a higher tuition fee than you charge for a teleseminar.

Create products. Record your webinars, and you will instantly begin building a collection of products. Webinars may be sold as stand-alone training courses. Record enough, and you will be able to offer your clients access to an entire library of relevant, results-oriented training programs – available on demand, so they can learn from you at their convenience. In essence, there is a passive income opportunity to be leveraged as well.

Keep the revenue flowing. Rather than saying good-bye at the end of your keynote and consulting engagements, attendee-funded webinars give you a way to nurture the relationship and help your audience commit and implement your teachings. Continuing your clients' education in the form of AFWs that dive deeply into specific components of your teachings creates an expanded, and ongoing, revenue relationship. They get a taste in the keynote speech and a new appetite is developed.

Book more speaking engagements. If you are like most speakers, trainers, and consultants, you have prospects who are interested in hiring you to deliver a keynote, train their employees, or provide consulting services. Showing them a taped speech is one way to demonstrate your expertise. Far more compelling is inviting them to participate in your webinar, because they will experience first-hand what it is like to be in your audience. The registration fee can help to separate serious prospects from tire-kickers. After all, if they aren't willing to invest a few bucks to experience you in action, how serious are they about working with you?

Increase your visibility. The more diverse forms of training you offer, the greater your prospect reach. In-person seminars and workshops are ideal solutions for a certain segment of your audience. Others will never attend an in-person event, no matter how well you market it or how fairly it's priced. While some companies are gung-ho about bringing speakers and trainers into their organizations, others are working with limited budgets or busy schedules, making on-site training nearly impossible. By adding virtual training programs to your portfolio, you are able to reach those who were outside your grasp with only an in-person option for your services.

Establish expertise and credibility. Just as publishing a book elevates you to the level of expert in the eyes of the public, becoming a speaker or trainer helps establish your expertise in the eyes of many of your prospects. If you already deliver speeches and presentations, adding eLearning to your mix further solidifies this perception and expands your credibility. The more topics and modes of delivery you use, the more you increase your audience's perception of you as an experienced, well-rounded thought leader.

Position yourself as cutting edge - and stay current. In the Information Age, prospects expect thought leaders and experts to stay on the cutting edge of technology. For speakers, trainers and consultants, staying current means delivering virtual training to be on the leading edge. The message communicated by offering virtual training courses is that what you teach isn't "yesterday's news." It's designed to help you solve today's and tomorrow's challenges.

Satisfy more clients. A certain segment of your audience will always desire a lower-priced option than in-person training events and presentations. Others simply don't have the time or interest to participate in seminars or workshops. Still others prefer live interaction with you, but are seeking ways to reduce their training expenses in light of the economic downturn. Adding virtual training to your mix gives you a way to satisfy all of these consumers.

Lower your risk. Using in-person training events to roll out new content or to introduce you as a speaker in the marketplace can be a risky venture. Depending on your costs for room rental, audiovisual equipment, food and beverage, registration staff, event planning and management, and even sleeping rooms, you could be committed to spending hundreds or thousands of dollars. You've committed to this huge expenditure without even knowing if there is an audience that will pay for your content. Virtual training events give you an easy, low-risk way to test your content. Your expenses are considerably lower, making it easier to profit from your virtual training venture. As an added plus, if registration levels miss their mark, it will not be obvious to participants that your event is not the smashing success you had hoped it would be. Ten people in a ballroom is an embarrassment, but ten people in your AFW is invisible to the attendees and profitable for you!

Lower stress. One of the biggest stresses and frustrations with offering your own training events is trying to guess how many registrations you will receive – and then handling a last-minute flood of registrations. Virtual training eliminates this hassle. If your event is a smashing success, you will be able to handle the increased capacity without worrying about procuring a larger meeting room or being able to adjust your food and beverage requirements at the last minute. You provide the training; they bring the vittles.

Enhance the sales conversation. Delivering training that makes a measurable impact on your clients' lives is the best way to persuade them that they need to continue working with you. The next step in your relationship might be a webinar series or an in-person workshop. It might be a consulting or coaching arrangement. In any case, you will find it easier to sell prospects on other services after they have witnessed the power of a short, results-oriented webinar with you.

Although there always will be a place for in-person seminars and workshops, virtual training is not a fad. If you want to continue to be perceived as an expert, to remain relevant and in-demand, and to grow your revenue, you need to add AFWs to your product offering. It's not a matter of "if"; it's a matter of "when."

2 | Straddling the Fine Line Between Free and For-Fee

Develop a Webinar That Prospects Will Gladly Pay to Attend

Don't get me wrong. This book is not a damning of free webinars. Far from it! Free webinars can have their place in your marketing and product development mix. They increase your exposure and name recognition, while also generating leads for your business and building your database of names. The challenge for most speakers is the lack of a strategy to monetize their free webinars. This results in giving away their proprietary information with exposure as their only compensation. I'm not sure if you have tried going to the bank with an "exposure deposit," but it doesn't work overly well. If you want to generate revenue, especially during lean times when your in-person speaking and training opportunities are limited, attendee-funded webinars (AFWs) are for you.

One of the key decisions you must make is the type of content you will deliver in your virtual presentation. This is not a quick decision as it will have a major affect on your success with AFWs. The general public has been trained to expect certain types of webinars to be offered for free. If you want to develop AFWs as a viable revenue stream, you need to offer an event for which your audience is willing to open its collective wallet. Let's take a look at the different types of webinars ... and which are appropriate for charging tuition and which are expected to be delivered for free.

Book-based. If you've written a book, the knee-jerk reaction to the AFW opportunity is to say "I'll deliver a webinar based on my book...and I'll even give the webinar the same title." If that's your intent, welcome to the world of free events. People are not going to pay to hear an overview of your book. When they see that your webinar is really an infomercial designed to persuade people to buy a copy of your book, they may even resent your request to pay for it. Think about it from their perspective. If your book is 200 pages long, how much content can you cover adequately in an hour? If you covered 5%, you would be lucky.

That said, a book is a wonderful launching device for moving into the attendee-funded webinar space. Instead of trying to encompass all of the content you present in the book, select a single chapter to focus on during your webinar. Take a deep dive into the content beyond what you have covered in the book, and help the participants – who may or may not have your book – implement your teachings. By doing so, you have gone from being an author to being a trainer – and people expect to pay for training. The other good news is that by leading a deeper exploration into the topic of your book, you're able to expand your webinar offering from a single, broad-reaching event to multiple, content-rich ones. The more products you offer, the stronger your revenue opportunity will be.

Problem awareness. Let's say you have studied a problem from every vantage point and want to help your audience to become acutely aware of the problem and its impact. So, you decide to formulate an awareness-raising webinar so that attendees leave the event well-educated on the issue and its ramifications. Your goal is to instill participants with the desire to hire you to resolve the problem.

If this is your approach, welcome to the free webinar space! People will not pay for awareness of an issue. The marketplace is saturated with awareness-raising webinars – and they are free. If your goal is to build a database or drive sales, don't charge attendees to participate to ensure you accomplish your mission.

If you want your webinar to generate revenue from the event itself versus generating revenue in the form of sales after the event, special care must be given to the content structure and presentation. Remember, people will not pay to be made aware of a problem, but they will pay to learn how to resolve the challenges they face. If your webinar delivers the resolution, people will pay for the content. For example, if your webinar focuses on the impact of stress upon the body, productivity, and overall health, that is a free event. However, if the webinar teaches participants how to reduce the impact of stress so that they are healthier and more productive, it becomes an event you can sell.

Statistical report. Conducting research is expensive. If you have spent countless hours researching and studying a subject, you may be tempted to develop an AFW as a means to monetize the investment of time that you've made. As with the awareness-raising webinar model, the marketplace expects statistical data to be presented in webinars for free. In essence, a statistical webinar is very similar to an awareness webinar in that you are making the attendees aware of what you have found, but not telling them what to do about the data findings.

Although the information from your research is interesting and you are passionate about what you have found, prospective attendees generally will not pay for it. However, if you use the research to present hypotheses and help people understand how to implement what you have learned from your studies; you have crossed over to the attendee-funded marketplace.

For example, let's say that you have studied business communication and have developed a one-inch thick book of findings that illustrates the poor quality of business communication within U.S.-based organizations. You could present this data during a free webinar. If you want to charge a fee to participate in your webinar, you would explain the financial impact of poor communication in business and teach participants techniques to improve communication in the workplace.

Stories. As a speaker, you know that storytelling is a highly effective tool to use when delivering a keynote speech. Stories connect with, mesmerize and move audiences, which wins you rave reviews ... and ultimately, big speaking fees. However, although you get paid to deliver keynote speeches, you can't expect to take the same approach when delivering an AFW. It's possible to deliver a story-filled keynote speech and get paid because participants don't pay just to hear your stories; they get lunch and networking, too. If you want to deliver a webinar in which you'll primarily deliver stories, such as the biggest branding mistakes ever made in business, the public will expect your webinar to be a free event.

As with keynote speeches, stories make your webinar more interesting. If you want to charge attendees for your webinar, however, you need to take the next step. In conjunction with the stories, you need to teach participants what they should be doing to avoid making the same mistakes. As with the awareness webinar model, the storytelling webinar makes people aware of the problem, but doesn't tell people what to do about it. If the goal of your storytelling webinar is to build your database or generate product/service sales, keep the event gratis. If your goal is to generate income from registration fees, adjust your presentation strategy so that your stories are used to reinforce training points and teach skills, rather than serving as just entertainment.

Skill training. People are accustomed to paying for education and training. Virtual training is just another form of training. Webinars are simply a mechanism you can use to deliver your teachings to virtual audiences. If you structure your webinars for skill acquisition for the participants, you are ideally situated to pursue the AFW market. This requires covering a narrowly defined topic as thoroughly as possible to teach participants skills they can implement after your session.

For example, if you normally deliver a two-day, in-person training program, you could easily develop six to ten, one-hour training webinars from this content. For instance, if your area of expertise is sales management, you could deliver a multitude of webinars on sales compensation, recruiting and hiring sales people, driving sales productivity, etc. Even within each of those topics, you can create e-courses as a way to deliver your teachings in an AFW environment.

On the other hand, you might normally deliver a one- or two-hour overview seminar that presents the big-picture view of a problem and its solution. In this case, you could develop a series of webinars that examines each component of the solution in depth. For example, if your overview presentation discusses business management strategies, your webinars may provide insight into topics such as effective hiring, managing cash flow, and bringing out the best in your employees.

Is My Webinar Saleable?

Free	For-Fee
❏ Information	❏ Skill-based training
❏ General overview	❏ Narrowly focused content
❏ Based on a book	❏ A chapter or two from the book
❏ Issue awareness	❏ Problem with resolution techniques
❏ Statistical research	❏ Synthesized data to direct action
❏ Stories	❏ Stories used as a lead-in to resolve a challenge

Selecting Your Topic

Now that you understand the depth and breadth of the content that should be included in AFWs, it's time to begin identifying the topics that you can present. Many speakers with whom I consult can teach multiple topics and require guidance to determine which ones are most saleable. My advice is this:

Think about the requests for assistance that you have received from clients in the last three to six months. What did your clients ask of you? What themes were you able to pinpoint relative to their needs?

The answers to these questions will lead you to the topics you should consider developing for AFW delivery. Why? First, there is obviously a current demand for this training which is not being fulfilled. The requests you receive are evidence of the demand. Second, and equally important, you are recognized as having an expertise in the subject matter, as they came to you for assistance.

To further identify and flesh out your ideas for potential AFW topics, here are five introspective questions. (Each question is followed by a sample response.)

1. **What are the top challenges plaguing my clients today?**

    Revenue is down, causing profitability pain.

2. **Why do they struggle with this problem or frustration?**

    While the economy is part of the reason for this dynamic, there are a number of things business leaders should be doing under any economic conditions to ensure profitability.

3. **What actions do they need to take to solve the problem?**

    They need to learn how to price their services correctly, manage cash flow and allocate staff based on metrics.

4. **What individual skills do they need to master in order to accomplish these tasks?**

    They need to learn how to review the reports in order to transform them into direct action. This includes learning how to read a P&L beyond the numbers, reviewing all of the costs associated with providing their services, and correlating both of these to staffing.

5. After developing the list of skills that are necessary to solve the problem, consider what additional skills must be learned first or would make learning these new skills easier?

Learning to build a staffing model for a service-based business would be a helpful pre-requisite for attendees to ensure they can leverage the skills from this training.

Do You Have the Credentials to Teach the Course?

I recall talking with a speaker about work-life balance issues and suddenly having a revelation. The work-life balance issue had taken a new turn based on the economic challenges that required managers to take a different approach. I could see it clear as day. Boy, I was chomping at the bit to deliver this webinar. However, I don't have the credentials to teach it. I'm not a human resources expert, nor am I a psychologist, nor a social worker. While the opportunity was staring me in the face with huge dollar signs dancing in my head, I had no business teaching it. I don't have the credentials to teach the course, which means no one is going to buy it.

Similarly, you may identify topics that you'd like to teach or you know your target audience needs ... but you don't have the requisite credentials. Although nearly all speakers, trainers and consultants think that they are unique in what they do, the reality is that people have thousands of choices from whom to learn about any topic. If you want to convert prospects into registrants, you need to be able to answer their question of "Why you? Of all of the people in the world who offer this, why are you the person from whom I should learn these skills?"

Before committing to teaching an AFW, it's important to objectively evaluate your demonstrable expertise. During the process of converting prospects to paid webinar registrants, your bio will come into play. If your credentials do not support what you are teaching, prospective registrants will decide that your AFW is not worth an investment of their time and money. The webinar topic gets their attention, but your credentials seal the deal.

When deciding whether you appear to be a qualified presenter, prospects will consider your:

- Education and training
- Work experience
- Client feedback (testimonials)
- Books and articles written
- Lecturing and speaking experience
- Certifications and licenses
- Longevity in a particular field

"But what about my personal experience?" you might be asking. For example, let's say you want to offer an AFW to teach future entrepreneurs what to expect when starting their own business. Your only credential is the fact that you run your own business. You don't have any other credentials, such as an advanced business degree or experience helping other entrepreneurs tackle this particular challenge. Is having personal experience with the topic you're teaching going to be enough to sell your event?

Yes and no. For some prospects, your personal accomplishments give you greater credibility than a distinguished professor with zero real-world experience. For other prospects, your lack of acceptable credentials, such as a related academic degree, professional experience, teaching experience and so on could make your expertise questionable. The more credentials you have – the more proof you can offer that you do – the easier it will be to sell virtual seats. The bottom line? Pick content that is in your bailiwick.

Why Learn This Topic Now?

This is one of my favorite discussions ... and I have it over 20 times a week with speakers. Every one of them has content that would be beneficial to learn. Their content is certainly important. You would be hard-pressed to find a professional speaker, consultant, or trainer whose content is not important. Yet, importance alone does not get people to sign up for AFWs. It doesn't drive them to take action.

Choosing a webinar topic that you're qualified to teach is not enough to ensure a successful event. When choosing a topic, the next step to selecting a saleable topic for your AFW is to analyze the sense of *urgency* around the issue you've identified.

To best convey how *importance* and *urgency* work, I took a page from Dr. Stephen Covey. In his time management book, *First Things First*, Covey presents a matrix that contrasts *importance* with *urgency*. His point is that you need to invest your time on items that are both *important* and *urgent*. When you apply this concept to AFWs, *importance* doesn't sell webinar seats. *Urgency* on its own doesn't sell seats either. However, when *importance* and *urgency* come together (I refer to this convergence as relevance), prospects become motivated to take action on the issue (i.e., pay for a seat in your webinar).

Imagine that you have been smoking for years. It is certainly important to stop smoking, but you aren't motivated to do so. Then, not feeling well, you go to the doctor who tells you that if you don't change your habits, the next time he sees you will be at your funeral. Now, *urgency* and *importance* have come together, and you will act.

Another way to look at this is through two words that I've used to help sales people drive sales – *synergy* and *priority*. *Synergy* is your ability to align your content with the needs of your target prospects. *Synergy* draws the attention of prospects in order to get them to look at what you have to offer. *Priority* answers the question of "Why now?" Think about all of the issues and problems that you or your business has at any one time. You aren't trying to solve all of your challenges simultaneously. You pursue resolution to those that are both *urgent* and *important*.

Sometimes what you teach is not *urgent* and *important* to the masses, so you must find a creative way to position your webinar. Imagine you are a sales trainer who teaches cold calling. Any business professional will tell you that cold calling is one of the most critical skills that a successful sales person must master. However, what makes it not only *important*, but also *urgent*, to master this skill? Clearly, it is an *important* skill to possess, but how do you position the course as both *urgent* and *important*? Start by analyzing the role that cold calling plays in the sales cycle – it's a primary way that salespeople generate leads. To make sales, you need to have sales meetings, and you can't schedule sales meetings without having people –prospects – with whom you can meet. Connecting the dots, by tying cold calling to the end result of making a sale, you position your AFW as both *important* and *urgent*. Every day that sales professionals do not master cold calling reduces the likelihood that they will meet their revenue targets.

To identify ways to make your webinar content *urgent* and not just *important*, return to my earlier advice and think about the last three to six months in your firm. When prospects called you for help, what assistance did they need? Can you identify a pattern? That pattern is the roadmap guiding you to what is hot now.

For instance, let's say you're a management expert. Clearly, there are many different courses you can teach in an AFW format. As you reflect on the last several months of discussions with clients and prospects, you recognize they are mainly contacting you to help restore employee trust following a workforce reduction. A ha! No more guesswork! There is demand (*imporant* and *urgent*) in the marketplace for you to teach this subject, and there is a perception that you are an expert since they are coming to you for guidance.

Go Broad or Go Narrow?

It would seem logical to create a webinar applicable for the biggest audience possible. The broader the scope, the more registrants you will have, right? Actually, the converse is true. With AFWs, the prospective registrant net is finite. With a broad-ranging topic, the net doesn't become larger; instead, the holes stretch and prospective attendees fall through them. When you try to create an AFW that appeals to everyone, the webinar description conveys "general" to prospective attendees – and they immediately write off the event as not being applicable to them. If you were going to invest money in training, would you pay for a session that was not specifically geared toward you and your needs? Probably not.

> A key to driving registrant conversion is to have narrow topics, but go deeply into the subject matter.

People aren't willing to pay to hear you gloss over a myriad of topics. They want substance! The content should target a very specific audience so the reader of your description says, "Hey! This is designed specifically for me!" ... and buys a seat in your virtual training event.

Imagine that you teach business writing, a topic that has been important since the days of hieroglyphics. Everyone agrees that business writing is an *important* skill, but on the surface, it's not also an *urgent* skill. Thus, if you offer this e-course to the masses, you will struggle to generate registrants. To successfully turn this topic into an AFW, you must find a way to make the topic *urgent*, as well. In this case, the key is an audience segmentation strategy. Ask yourself who would consider business writing to be both *important* and *urgent* today.

One audience segment that comes to mind is sales people. Sales people are always looking for a way to differentiate themselves with prospects. Although most sales professionals are known for mastering the gift of gab, few have the same impact when they are tasked with taking the relationship to paper. Yet, if there is going to be a revenue relationship with the prospect (i.e., getting the business), at some point the relationship must be memorialized in writing. The business writing AFW described above could be geared specifically to sales people looking for a competitive edge. This approach allows you to focus on a specific audience that has a very specific problem which you can solve with your teachings. And *voila!* It makes the webinar both *urgent* and *important*. In this case, you aren't selling business writing to sales people. You are selling a tool that gives them a leg up on the competition.

That's just one market segment. Who else needs to learn business writing today? We know that many companies have experienced a workforce reduction. Thus, trust among the remaining employees has been damaged. Emails that come from corporate are not greeted by "What does it say?" Employees think "What does it

REALLY say?" Imagine an AFW for managers of companies that have experienced a workforce reduction in which they learn how to communicate with email so that the message that is received is the message that is intended. In this case, business writing is not what the attendee is buying. He is buying tools to help him rebuild trust and credibility with his team.

Now, this speaker has two e-courses for two audience types for which the positioning is both *urgent* and *important*. The courses align well with the focus of the target audience. From the speaker's perspective, there is another key benefit. The majority of what is taught in the two events – core business writing concepts – is identical. The difference between the two events is the webinar description and the examples used in the webinar. More revenue-producing events with minimal content development ... it doesn't get much better than that!

Let's examine negotiation as another potential AFW topic. If you put together a negotiation virtual training course, it will be difficult to convert attendees. Why? Negotiation is a huge topic with many applications. After reading your webinar description, prospects will feel your AFW is too general and won't address their specific needs.

To make this topic more saleable, consider the many applications of negotiation and develop AFWs for those, such as: negotiation for business-to-business sales people ... or negotiation for procurement agents ... or negotiation for hiring managers. The core content is negotiation, but you are simply applying this core to different markets. By being registrant-centric, you will convert attendees at a higher rate and be able to offer additional revenue-generating sessions.

There is another important benefit – greater reach. First, each time you customize a webinar to a particular audience, you expand your product line. This will increase your reach as you go out to secure additional speaking engagements and even consulting work. An organization that would overlook your "generic" presentation may give you a second look when an executive sees that you offer a program specifically for its members, employees or industry. Think big picture here: AFWs open the door to consulting, in-person training, and speaking engagements in a variety of industries. As the expert leading the webinar, you are perceived as having content specifically tailored to this audience.

Develop a Series or Offer Stand-Alone Courses?

Assuming that you will offer more than one AFW in your lifetime, another consideration to keep in mind is how to organize your line-up of virtual training events. Should you handle each event as stand-alone content, or should each session build from the previous webinar? Both approaches have their pros and cons.

Structuring your AFWs as a series allows you to take a group of people through a developmental process. This improves the chances of producing remarkable case studies and strong testimonials from your participants. Working with the same group during ten, one-hour webinars affords you the opportunity to convey a deeper level of skill transfer. This, presumably, translates into significant changes that produce measurable results. Offering a webinar series also allows you to charge for the entire program upfront, which helps your cash flow and creates audience commitment.

The downside to offering a series – especially when earlier programs are a prerequisite to later events – is that once the train has left the station, it's gone. Once you've started the program, new prospects cannot sign up, resulting in lost revenue.

Stand-alone webinars give you the flexibility to develop a diverse virtual training catalog. You can develop a wider range of topics and reach different audiences for each webinar. By taking this approach, you may find that you can deliver AFWs more frequently. You are targeting different audiences versus repeatedly marketing to the same people. It also allows attendees to sign up at any time for your webinars without worrying about prerequisites.

The disadvantage of this approach is that you rely on "single sales." Because each webinar is its own product, each webinar needs to be promoted separately. You may find it more laborious to promote several individual events versus a series.

A third option is to offer both types of AFWs. People who are looking for comprehensive teachings can build their knowledge and skills with a webinar series, while prospects who want specific content on a finite subject can attend a modular program.

It is important to note that the duration of the webinar affects your price point. If you are delivering a 30-minute AFW, you should not use the same price point as a 60-minute one. Later, when reviewing the webinar back-office provider selection process, this may impact your decision on webinar length. It may cost you as much to deliver 30 minutes of content as it does 60 minutes, but with the shorter event, you would receive less revenue.

To maximize sales of your AFWs, you must take a unique approach to developing your webinar course strategy. A key to successfully selling your virtual seats is the delivery of topics that are aligned with the focus of your target registrants and diving deeply into the content so they acquire the skills to succeed.

Price Drivers

One of the big challenges that you face is what to charge for your AFW. There are no steadfast rules here. The range that I've found is between $25 and $500 per registrant for a one-hour AFW. Here are some considerations when developing your pricing.

1. **Per Connection vs. Per Person.** One negative about AFWs is that you have no control over who is watching the webinar. There is nothing that prevents someone from putting the webinar on a projector, the phone on conference, and inviting the 10-person sales team to participate. Keep this in mind when you set your pricing. In this instance, a $100 webinar is only $10 per person. Since you can't control access, don't discourage it. Price your webinar so that you account for this dynamic.

2. **Value.** If you set the price too low, prospects will assume that your AFW does not have much value. Develop a price that is in line with the value of your time and the results your teachings will provide. Remember, this is a webinar, not a teleseminar, so you can easily justify a higher price point.

3. **Recording.** If you include a recording of your webinar with the registration fee, you can command a higher fee as this allows registrants to watch your webinar again. If this were a seminar, they wouldn't have that opportunity.

4. **Early registration.** Since most registrants enroll within 48 hours of the webinar, you may want to drive the behavior of early enrollment. You can offer a discount for signing-up early (i.e., enroll more than two days before the webinar, you save 10%.)

5. **Group registration.** You'd love to have as many people as possible enroll for your webinar. To encourage multiple registrations from a group, you can offer a discount for multiple registrants. (i.e., Enroll three employees and save 15%.)

6. **Giveaways.** Another factor to consider when setting your price is what you are including in the registration fee. For example, if you are including a 15-minute consult and your billable rate is $200 per hour. This has a $50 value.

7. **Credits.** If you pursue the option of providing Continuing Education Units (CEUs) or some other type of credit for your AFW, you can justify a higher price point.

3 | Understanding the Webinar Buying Process

How Prospects Evaluate Virtual Training Courses ... and Who Ultimately Buys Them

As with any effective product sale, a key area of study is the way in which prospects buy. In this case, how your prospects buy attendee-funded webinars (AFWs) – what they look for when evaluating training, who makes the buying decision, and when they buy are areas for analysis.

People attend in-person events for a variety of reasons, ranging from rubbing elbows with an expert, to gaining access to an elite group of forward-thinking professionals, from learning cutting-edge information, to networking with colleagues and prospective clients. The driving force behind AFWs is vastly different than in-person events.

As discussed earlier, the primary reason people participate in AFWs is the acquisition of new skills for themselves or their teams. Even though basic content could be attained online or in a book, there are many people who prefer an instructor-led learning environment. For example, although it's possible to learn how to set up a WordPress blog by reading a book and using online resources, some people will attend an AFW to learn this skill. They are lured by the instructor's implied promise to teach them, step-by-step, how to do something they don't have the time, skill, or patience to learn on their own. In other cases, attendees are looking for cutting-edge expertise, and they'll be attracted by the opportunity to acquire skills that will give them the upper hand.

Another reason your prospects may be enticed to participate in your AFW is that it provides a relatively low-cost, low-risk way to familiarize themselves with your content, as well as your teaching style. If you offer big-ticket products, services or events, a webinar provides a great way for prospects to check you out before making the bigger investment. If they enjoy and receive value from a 60-minute AFW which teaches techniques for getting past gatekeepers, it becomes easier for them to see your one-day seminar on cold calling as a smart investment.

People become qualified prospects for your webinar when they identify a problem that they want to solve. Problems come with different levels of *urgency*, ranging from a goal they want to achieve, in which case the "problem" is merely not having the knowledge or skills to achieve the goal, to a crisis that needs to be addressed quickly to avoid dire consequences, such as not being able to meet payroll. Here are some common scenarios:

- "I need to enhance the organizational skills of my employees to increase productivity."

- "I need training so I can better perform my duties."

- "We are not getting the performance we need from our team and need to help them boost their productivity."

- "We need to get in front of more prospects. How can we reach qualified prospects without spending more on sales?"

- "Our company is bleeding cash. We need to figure out how to stop it – fast!"

- "Our customer service department gets bad grades. We need to fix how the staff interacts with customers – we can't afford to lose more business."

- "I want to do my job better and am willing to invest in my continuing education."

- "I've been laid off. Now would be a great time to learn a new skill."

- "More layoffs are coming. It's essential that we keep morale and productivity up."

- "My industry is changing. I need training to stay up to date so I don't get left behind."

Marketing to Fans, Strangers, and Acquaintances

When promoting AFWs, there is a broad spectrum of prospects. At one end are those who know you well (*Fans*) and at the other end of the spectrum are those who are unfamiliar with you (*Strangers*). In the middle of the spectrum are those who have had some introduction to you, but you don't have controlled access to them (*Acquaintances*). The process for converting each of these groups is vastly different.

Fans are always the first ones pursued for your AFWs, but many speakers make a strategic error with this group. To help you avoid this – *implementing the teachings in this book and then concluding "I followed your teachings to the letter, but no one from my database signed-up for my webinar. AFWs don't work for me"* – let's pull back the curtain and show you what happens when I conduct marketing post-mortems on AFWs that didn't generate the expected sales.

The webinar post-mortem begins with a simple question: "How did your prospects get into your database?"

The typical answer: "Oh, I've been teaching this material in-person for years. I've used this content to build my database."

Interesting, isn't it? After all, how many times would you pay to learn the same thing? The message: Just because delivering your presentation via webinar is new to you; don't expect your *Fans* to pay again to hear you present the same content a second time.

Clients who subscribed to your database because you dazzled

them with past teachings are ideal prospects for an AFW, but not for the same content. After all, they obviously liked how and what you taught and will pay for the privilege of learning from you again. They will not buy the same course again just because it is being presented using a different medium. The key to success with *Fans* is offering them something new, but related to their experience with you.

What can you do? Go back to Chapter 2 and review the process for choosing an AFW topic for which your registrants will gladly pay. A few ideas to contemplate -

- If you have delivered level 101 training, develop a level 201 program to deliver as an AFW.

- If you already offer a comprehensive training program in your subject of expertise, use your webinar to laser-focus on one area and take them on a deep-dive into that content. For example, if you normally deliver sales training, use your webinar to teach sales professionals how to conduct an effective needs analysis discussion. If you normally teach marketers how to write effective copy, use your webinar to teach the finer points of writing a compelling headline.

Coming back to our post-mortem webinar discussion, sometimes the discussion gets even more frightening. After being asked how many times they would pay to learn the same content, the speaker responds by saying, "Oh no, I didn't charge for that the first time. It was a free seminar." By delivering this AFW, speakers are, in essence, asking their *Fans* to pay for something that they have already given away for free. If you attempt this approach, not only will they refuse to pay to attend your AFW, but they will also resent your request to pay for a gift you have given them in the past.

When you are able to develop webinar content significantly different from, or more advanced than, prior trainings – and you can successfully communicate these key differences to your *Fans* – you will be able to leverage your relationship with them. They already know who you are and what you do, and they like your work. If your relationship is strong, a fair number of *Fans* may register for your webinar, even if your webinar description is weak. In fact, some *Fans* may sign up for your AFW knowing nothing more than the webinar title or topic, as long as they can grasp the difference and benefit of your new virtual course.

As you implement the AFW program into your business, it is critical that you make a careful decision about what content you will deliver for free versus attendee-funded. Once you condition your *Fans* to expect content-rich training from you for free, it becomes difficult to flip the switch to attendee-funded events. If free webinars serve a strategic purpose for your business, by all means, continue to use them. However, if you want to be successful in the AFW space, you need to make some critical business decisions about where you draw the line between free and for-fee.

If you want to maximize your registrations and drive mass AFW registrations, you need to have a strategy to reach beyond your *Fans*. Marketing to people who are not familiar with you, *Strangers*, is an entirely different game from marketing to your *Fans*, but obviously it is a much larger potential audience. Much of what is addressed in this book is geared toward being successful reaching the entire spectrum of prospective registrants. There are a few additional challenges to keep in mind as you seek to convert AFW registrants from the *Strangers* group:

Lack of familiarity. The people to whom you're marketing are not familiar with you. Because they generally won't recognize your name, you'll have to work smarter to grab their attention. Their lack of trust means you'll also need to be more strategic to win the registration.

Increased competition. When you're promoting to the general public, you'll face much greater competition for your prospects' attention. You'll be competing against other speakers who present the same topic. You'll be competing against other experts in your industry who are working hard to persuade prospects that their approach is most *important* and *urgent* for overall success.

No guarantee of repeat access. When promoting to your *Fans*, you have virtually unlimited access (minus the few people who unsubscribe every time you send an email) because you have their contact information. When promoting to the general public, there is no guarantee you'll ever see them or talk to them again. If they are not hooked the first time they see your promotion, they'll walk away forever.

To succeed when promoting AFWs to *Strangers*, your marketing materials need to grab their attention, establish your credentials, and help you stand out from the crowd. This is where many speakers get into trouble and their AFW venture fails.

Marketing to your *Fans* can lull you into a false sense of security. Because people who already like your work tend to be more responsive to your training offers, it's easy to become lax with the quality of the promotional materials you create. After all, they know you and have experienced you before. It's easy to forget that other people won't know your full story, credentials and background. You can lose sight of the fact that a person reading about you for the first time isn't intimately familiar with your branded terminology and verbiage. The shorthand that works when talking to your *Fans* can confuse and even turn off *Strangers*.

Later sections of this book address the various factors that affect your success when marketing to the public, including event title, subtitle, topic, webinar description, testimonials, and your credibility on the subject matter ... to name a few. The rule of thumb when promoting to the general public is to keep your marketing materials linear. Everything you share – about your expertise, your clients, your background and so on – must point to the conclusion that you are the subject matter expert from whom prospects should learn this skill.

Business professionals often are counseled to think broadly to maximize reach and appeal. But showcasing your vast range of experience and expertise can backfire when promoting your AFW. Instead, ensure that all of the materials position you as a thought leader on a particular subject matter.

For example, if you are delivering a management AFW, your bio should convey an expertise in resolving management challenges. The testimonials you use should reflect your clients' experiences in working with you on management issues. Articles you write should position you as a management expert. Everything should form a straight line that ends in an arrow pointing to you and your expertise as a management expert. In essence, your virtual training event is really a focused campaign. All else should be set aside for a different promotion or, at the very least, drastically downplayed.

With hundreds, if not thousands, of competitors, you cannot afford to have any chinks in your armor. If your bio fails to support your expertise on the subject matter, you will struggle to convert attendees. If your testimonials don't reinforce your expertise on this subject, you will have challenges generating registrations. If your articles don't demonstrate your expertise on your webinar topic, you will fail to achieve the registration results you seek. Think of all the components of a successful webinar promotion as puzzle pieces. They all must fit perfectly into place to be effective.

The Middle of the Prospective Registrant Spectrum

Another valuable prospect group to leverage in order to drive registrations to your AFWs is one to which you do not have direct access. They have had some experience with you, but you don't have their contact information. *Acquaintances* are the audiences from your prior speaking engagements such as association members.

Associations are always on the lookout for two things ... more services for their members and non-dues revenue. Your AFWs satisfy both of these objectives.

Think of the associations for which you have spoken ... maybe even for free. The members have enjoyed some experience with you. They are a great potential source for registrations for your AFWs. Offer the association a commission for the registrations they generate.

Another way to approach the association opportunity is to consider those in which you are already a member. As one who has paid dues, you may find the association willing to promote your AFWs to the other members.

Don't underestimate the importance of *Acquaintances*. They will be more likely to register for your AFWs than *Strangers* since the first time they heard about the webinar isn't the first time they heard of you. There is gold to be mined from this group!

Prospective AFW Registrants

	Fans	Acquaintances	Strangers
Who are they?	Your clients Newsletter database Close colleagues	Former keynote speech audiences Fellow association members Business networks	General public
Registrant Conversion Strategy	Offer them <u>new</u> content	Leverage their prior experience with you	Demonstrate thought leadership
Registrant Challenge	Positioning *urgency* and *importance*	Reaching them	Establishing trust and credibility
Access	Controlled	Limited	One-time

How Different Audiences Read Your AFW Description

Understanding the two ends of the prospective registrant spectrum are important when raising awareness and generating interest in your AFW. There are also two prospect types within the categories who will evaluate your AFW, but with vastly different criteria.

Prospective buyers evaluate your AFW from a Return-on-

Investment perspective. It's important to note that the buyer is sometimes the attendee, but not always. At other times, the buyer is a manager who either is procuring training for his or her employees or reviewing an employee's request to spend company dollars on training.

Prospective attendees will focus on what you'll teach and how they benefit from it. They know what problem they want to solve and will be reading the AFW description to see if you are the one to help them solve it.

The Webinar Registration Curve

The final element of the buying process that requires your attention is the registration timeline for AFWs.

When marketing any type of event, in-person or virtual, the number of registrations you receive on a daily basis increases as your event draws closer. The result is a registration curve that looks like a fishhook, with a dramatic increase in the last days before the event. Over time, it's possible to identify a registration pattern for a particular event, which enables seminar promoters to predict the total number of attendees a month or two before their events based solely on the buying pattern.

With an in-person event, you'll often receive most of your registrations in the last two to three weeks before the event.

With free webinars, registrations will come in with the first promotion – even if your first promotion is launched four weeks before the webinar date. This is due to the lack of commitment required to participate in a free webinar. Because prospects will not lose anything if they decide at the last minute not to participate, they'll sign up for the free webinar, but only a few show up. As few as 25% of registrants will actually attend the free webinar -- for the same reason they were able to sign up so easily -- there is no registration fee to lose if they don't show up. They have no skin in the game.

With an AFW, a full **50 to 75% of your registrations will arrive in the last 48 hours** before the webinar – with some attendees registering just minutes before your event begins.

Read that again! This buying pattern will affect your entire promotional campaign.

The reason prospects wait until the last minute to register for AFWs is scheduling. With an in-person event, attendees sign up days in advance because they need to make arrangements to be away from the office and travel to your seminar. Once participants make the decision to attend, they go into Outlook and mark themselves "out-of-office" for that day. They've committed!

With AFWs, the decision-making process is almost the complete opposite. Webinars don't require the same level of advanced planning. Because webinars are short and don't require participants to leave the office, potential participants don't clear their calendars days, weeks or months in advance as they do with in-person seminars. Instead, they tend to keep their options open, signing up as long as nothing else takes that time in their schedule, such as a meeting or conference call.

When prospective registrants read your AFW description though, all they think is, "Wow! This looks really interesting ... and if I don't have a meeting or a conference call at this time, I'm definitely going to attend." When do they know that their schedule is free? It's usually the day before or day of your webinar ... which is when they sign up for your event.

To effectively promote – and sell – your AFW virtual seats, you must keep this behavioral driver in mind by building your marketing calendar around your prospects' tendency to register at the last minute. In other words, start promoting early to raise awareness of your event, but increase the frequency and urgency of your promotions as your AFW gets closer. The real value of early promotion is to raise awareness of your event and, with luck, motivate prospects to write a note on their calendars to tentatively reserve time to participate. If you want to promote your AFW more than two weeks in advance, use messaging that is less promotional and more newsworthy or informational. We'll delve into AFW campaigns later.

Before selecting the tools that you will use to contact your prospects, you first need an effective, well-crafted AFW description. This tool will serve as the foundation for all other promotional materials you create.

4 | Designing the Scope of Your Webinar

Create the Framework for Your Virtual Event with 8 Key Questions

Now that you've seen the opportunity afforded by attendee-funded webinars (AFWs), you probably want to jump in and write your program description. Before you can design an effective AFW description, you need to first gather the building materials needed to construct it.

The following AFW Description Creator™ walks you through a step-by-step process to help you easily formulate a clear picture of the scope of your event.

> To access the AFW Description Creator™ worksheet, visit StopSpeakingForFree.com and enter AFW4ME.

1. What Are You Going to Teach in the Session?

A great starting point is to compose a one-paragraph summary of what you will teach and how learning this content will benefit the participants. This step provides the overall direction for your AFW, which will be useful as you develop the rest of the copy.

> *In this webinar, I will teach small business owners how to find costs that are weighing down their business and reducing their profitability. With those identified, I'll present a methodology to analyze each cost to determine its necessity.*

2. What Skills Will Be Acquired in the Webinar?

The operative word here is *skills*. Remember, awareness and informational webinars are not saleable. People will pay for transference of skills that help them improve and succeed.

Make a list of the skills that attendees will learn through participation in your virtual training course. An easy way to compile this list is to complete the statement: "You will learn how to _____."

After writing this list, review the promises you've made and ask yourself whether it is truly feasible to teach an attendee how to do the things you've promised in the time allotted for your AFW. If not, you risk having your event perceived as an awareness-building event rather than a pure learning experience. If that happens, it will alienate potential registrants who resent being asked to pay for a webinar that doesn't deliver meaningful value and measurable results.

To make your AFW worth the investment, you must promise value – but not so much that your offer appears incredulous. If your webinar appears too broad, participants won't believe that you are going to take them on a deep dive into the content.

Aim to identify five to eight skills, and be specific as possible when describing what, exactly, will be taught in the session. Don't worry about writing these points in a "marketing style" for now – just document the skills in a straightforward manner.

3. Who Is the Target <u>Buyer</u> and Who Is the <u>Attendee</u>?

Earlier, I shared the distinction between the buyer and attendee. Remember, sometimes the buyer of your AFW is not the same person as the attendee, depending on what you are teaching in the session. When it comes time to write the AFW description, the message you create should be geared toward both the buyer and the attendee.

For example, imagine you were teaching an AFW about time management designed for employees in companies that have reduced their workforce. The target attendees are the employees, but it is highly unlikely that they will buy this session. Instead, the target buyers are the business owners or executives who made the tough decision to downsize the workforce and recognize that the company has asked its employees to do more with less. They want to equip employees with skills that allow them to handle their new, expanded workload. In this case, the AFW description needs to be primarily focused on the target buyer, which becomes extremely important in the next sections of the description.

Buyers will read your webinar description and ask, "How will this training help me or my employees improve their skills? Is it worth my company's investment?" Buyers look not only at how the individual attending the training will benefit, but also at how the organization as a whole will benefit. Approving managers must ensure that their company's limited training dollars are spent in areas that will produce a maximum return on investment.

Ask yourself the following questions to start identifying ways that an organization will benefit from enrolling employees in your training. Will the company ...

- Increase revenue?
- Increase profits?
- Cut costs?
- Boost productivity?
- Expand market share?
- Retain more customers?
- Improve team morale?
- Reduce conflict?
- Increase customer or employee retention?
- Shorten the sales cycle?
- Reduce mistakes and errors?

If you answered "yes" to any of these questions, go one step further and identify whether you have any statistics or examples share to support these claims. If you do, use them. The specifics you provide will make your claims more believable ... and make your e-training more compelling.

4. What Problem Are You Solving for Both the Buyer and the Attendee?

Think about what you are teaching in your webinar – what challenge does your AFW address? Consider this question from the buyer's perspective, as well as from the attendee's perspective. You know what skills you'll be teaching – think about how attendees will be able to apply these skills. Afterall, application is the highest form of learning. It's important to identify the problems that attendees will be able to solve with the skills you teach and how solving them is relevant to the buyer. People are most receptive to paying for an AFW when they are actively seeking a solution to a problem. If you can show that your teachings will help to solve a front-of-mind issue for the buyer and/or attendee, they will be willing to invest in the solution your AFW provides.

Let's look again at the example of a time management AFW. The problem you solve for the employee is very different than the problem being solved for management. Your content will help employees reduce stress and get their work done. Management sees an opportunity to improve efficiency, productivity, and profitability.

In our society, most employees feel it is the responsibility of their employers to help them improve job proficiency. Few make the personal financial investment to increase job performance. For example, if you are teaching sales people how to effectively cold call, few sales people will buy your AFW. Your goal should be for the manager to purchase the AFW for her sales people as a training course. The manager will buy this to increase sales. The attendees will see this more narrowly as a skill improvement opportunity.

5. What Is the Impact of Inaction?

We all have issues and problems, but we're not trying to solve them all right now. Instead, we prioritize the problems that present the biggest threat if left unresolved. To demonstrate to prospects that your AFW is both *important* and *urgent*, you need to help them recognize that the problem you'll solve is both *important* and *urgent*. So identify what could or would happen if the aforementioned issue is not solved immediately. Again, it is the buyer whom you are trying to engage, more so than the attendee.

Imagine you are a speaker who instructs business consultants how to grow their business. You share with them that business consulting is a $100 billion industry, yet they may be struggling to get a morsel of revenue. The potential impact of not making the smart decision to participate in your webinar is straightforward. If they don't immediately learn how to grow their business, they may need to shut it down and find a job. The impact pulls at the emotional strings of the reader and generates action!

6. Why Should I Learn How to Solve This Problem From You?

Remember, prospects have choices from which they can select to improve their skills. To show them that they should learn this content from you, it's essential to position yourself as a thought leader on the topic.

When writing your AFW description, you will need to present your "wow!" – what makes you a unique, if not the best, trainer for this particular subject. The question to ask yourself is what are your two most compelling, powerful, relevant credentials pertinent to this subject matter? As you compile your list of credentials, consider what your criteria would be in the selection of an expert from whom you would want to learn. In essence, what conveys expertise to a prospective registrant?

Effective and proven examples of expertise include:

- Having authored a book/articles on the subject
- Education and training
- Certifications
- Past and current clients
- Number of clients
- Years of experience
- Countries in which you have worked
- Industries in which you have experience

* Previous courses taught
* Training programs developed
* Honors and awards received

The next component of credibility is your bio. Stop! This isn't a cut-and-paste exercise from your website. You need a one-paragraph bio that concisely presents your expertise in this specific subject matter. This is not a generic representation of everything you have done in your career. It is a specific testament to your expertise in this subject. If your prowess doesn't come through in your bio, your competitor will get the registrant, not you.

Not sure that your bio is up to the task? Send your one-paragraph bio to a few colleagues for review. Solicit their honest feedback about what your bio says relative to your experise in the subject matter you plan to teach. If they don't immediately perceive you as a leading expert on the subject, go back to the drawing board and rewrite it.

The final component of credibility is *testimonials*. There have been a number of Internet conversion studies citing the importance of testimonials when it comes to enticing prospects to buy. But not just any testimonial will do. There is a formula for using testimonials to convert attendees in your AFWs, and the most powerful testimonials are:

Specific. Testimonials that rave about how wonderful you are may make you feel good, but they aren't effective when trying to convert attendees. The best testimonials describe how the participants benefited from working with you on this subject matter.

Relevant. If you are teaching a management webinar, but your testimonials support your sales expertise, not only will they not help you convert attendees, they will drive people away. It will look as if you're delivering content that you are not qualified to teach.

Brief. Again, a lengthy testimonial of your greatness will make you feel good, but it won't drive conversion. What matters is the relevance and importance of the comments being made pertaining to your topic. A concise, yet specific, testimonial of how you have impacted someone on this subject is best. Here is an example of a weak testimonial:

> *"This webinar was excellent! I'm glad I attended."*
> ~ Susie Smith, Executive Assistant, The Big Box Company

Here is an example of a strong testimonial supporting your claim that your AFW is a sound investment of time and money:

> *"I was surprised at how simple – and easy to implement – your time management system was. It took me less than an hour to make the needed changes to better process my tasks. Every day this week, I have completed everything on my to-do list – this is a first!"*
> ~ Susie Smith, Executive Assistant, The Big Box Company

In late 2009, the Federal Trade Commission published new guidelines regarding the use of testimonials and endorsements. Although I am not an attorney, I will summarize the new rules as this: be sure that the testimonials you use accurately describe the typical experience your clients have. Also, if you have testimonials from people who are paid to endorse your services, expertise or events, be sure to make their paid relationship clear. You can read full details about the new guidelines at:

http://www.ftc.gov/opa/2009/10/endortest.shtm

7. What Keywords Does Your Target Audience Use to Search Online for Solutions?

When people are searching the Internet for information about the problems you solve, what terminology are they using? The answer to this question becomes important when you are leveraging search engine optimization (SEO) and search engine marketing (SEM) to drive visibility to your AFWs.

Success in both SEO and SEM depends on your ability to identify the keywords your audience uses to search for your topic and then use those words in your AFW description. The more closely aligned your webinar description matches what prospects are looking for, the more successful you will be with search engine results. (SEO helps improve your rankings in organic searches, while SEM improves ranking in pay-per-click ads.) Use the Google AdWords Keyword Tool to identify your first and second most popular keywords or keyword phrases. At the time of printing, this tool can be accessed at:

https://adwords.google.com/select/KeywordToolExternal

8. How Can You Increase the Value of Your Event?

As a registrant conversion strategy, you may want to offer a give-away to those enrolling in your AFW. Examples of giveaways include e-books, audio books, tip sheets, and white papers. In essence, they are products that provide added value to your AFW attendees.

Giveaways increase the perceived value of your eLearning experience, making it easier to position it as a smart investment. You can also use giveaways to encourage prompt action, by offering the bonuses to the first certain number of registrants or to people who sign up by a certain deadline.

As with testimonials, use care when selecting giveaways. The giveaway should be pertinent to what you are teaching in the AFW and should have monetary value. Giving away an article or something that is readily available for free, particularly on your website, will not be helpful in your quest to convert attendees.

Now, you're ready for the next big step - the creation of your webinar description to drive registrations in your AFW. The next chapter takes you through the specialized copywriting design process for AFWs.

5 | Constructing Your Webinar Description

Write the Copy That Drives Registrations for Your Virtual Event

In the previous chapter, you gathered the building materials to write an effective attendee-funded webinar (AFW) description. Now, it's time to use those materials to construct a marketing tool that compels prospects to buy a seat in your virtual training event.

Don't underestimate the work you are about to do. The AFW description is your ultimate marketing tool to generate registrations. It creates the perception of the product. The buy/no-buy decision is going to be made based on what prospects read in that copy. While knowing your stuff is key to AFW attendee satisfaction, it doesn't make people register...the AFW description does.

Your AFW description serves as your around-the-clock sales force. In most cases, you won't be interacting personally with your prospective registrants. Instead, your webinar description must do the work of converting them into paid attendees. If your description is written using stiff, overly formal business language, it will be too dry to capture prospects' attention, much less close the sale. Likewise, if your description is full of marketing hyperbole, prospects will not recognize your webinar as a serious training and educational event.

This chapter will guide you through the development process of your AFW description using a specialized copywriting methodology. This methodology was created by applying basic sales concepts to writing an AFW description. Effective salespeople never begin a prospect meeting by lecturing on the greatness of their product. They conduct a needs analysis discussion with the prospect to develop the right solution. By contrast, many webinar descriptions are focused on what is being taught and fail to engage the reader. There is nothing in the copy that positions the problem that is being solved by participating in this webinar. Translation: No sale!

The AFW description methodology includes a title/subtitle, two paragraphs, five bullet points, and a giveaway. I'm going to share with you how this methodology works so you can visualize it. However, the way you read *is not how you write the webinar description*. This methodology is very important to keep in mind as you read this chapter. After presenting the methodology, you will be shown how to use the tools to construct your AFW description. An important thought to keep in mind throughout the AFW description development process is the keyword research you performed so that you use words/expressions that are found by the search engines.

Title/Subtitle

The AFW title serves an important purpose, not because it generates registrations, but rather because it grabs attention and entices prospects to read your webinar description. As famed advertiser David Ogilvy noted in *Ogilvy on Advertising*, "On average, five times as many people read the headlines as read the body copy. It follows that unless your headline positions your product; you have wasted 90% of your money."

In many cases, the webinar title serves as the promotional headline. If your title doesn't grab prospects' attention, you've lost them. But if your title does its job of grabbing a prospect's attention, it will generate enough interest to persuade them to read more.

AFW titles are especially important when your event is being listed alongside dozens of other AFWs and training programs. For example, if you are working with an eLearning provider to promote and deliver your AFWs, you could get lost in the crowd. Your webinar title is often the only piece of the AFW description prospects will see as they are browsing through the course catalog. If your title doesn't capture their attention, they won't read more about your event - and they won't register.

AFW Description Copywriting Methodology

TITLE / SUBTITLE	Conveys how to solve a specific problem for a finite audience
ISSUE	Presents the problem and its impact on the target audience
SOLUTION	Positions your experience and expertise in solving the problem; summarizes the benefits your webinar offers
TAKEAWAYS	Conveys the skills that will be acquired to address the problem
GIVEAWAY	Provides an extra incentive to enhance the value

The best AFW titles infer "how to." Since these are skill-based training sessions, your prospects want to learn how to do something. Fluffy titles that you may use for an article are not effective with AFWs. The title should clearly position what is being taught and the subtitle further fleshes out the concept presented in the title. The title grabs them, the subtitle moves them into a deeper reading of your copy, and the AFW description closes the deal.

To capture prospects' attention, your AFW title must scream "This event is for you!" To do this, incorporate one or more of the following approaches:

Topic or Content. It is best practice to include the topic of your AFW in the title. Try to be as specific as possible when presenting the topic. The more specific your content is, the more credible you are and the more unusual and compelling your training appears to be. For example, teaching a one-hour AFW on "Internet Marketing" is incredulous – it covers too broad a spectrum to be covered completely in a one-hour training course. Narrowing it down to a micro-topic, such as the basics of SEO or pay-per-click advertising, makes you more believable and helps garner interest.

Benefits. More specific benefits work best in the subtitle. Prospects are very busy and will not be reading your marketing copy word for word. Rather than making them do the mental work of figuring out how they'll benefit by learning the content you're going to teach, connect the dots for them. Identify and share a major benefit your training course will provide.

Target Audience. It is important to call out your target audience in either the title or subtitle as a means of engaging the right prospects. Earlier, you learned that two prospect types (buyer and attendee prospects) will read your AFW description. The webinar title (or subtitle) should address the attendee. Although you will want to address the buyer elsewhere in the copy, the webinar title should identify who should attend.

The three points outlined above will capture the interest of your readers. If you plan to use search engine marketing to drive traffic to your AFW promotion page, also consider what will attract the attention of search engines.

SEO Tip: If your AFW is being promoted on its own web page,

the webinar title can be used as the page title. The page title is one of the most important elements that search engines look for when determining the importance and relevance of your web page. To appeal to search engines, ensure that your webinar title is also the title tag, an SEO term. (The page title does not appear on the web page itself. Instead, it will appear at the very top of the browser window when a visitor lands on your web page.) Consult with your webmaster for assistance with putting this practice into place.

You'll know your AFW title is a winner if it passes this four-prong test:

1. If the target buyers read your title, would they know who should attend the event?
2. Would they understand what is being taught in this session?
3. Are enough benefits promised that they would be compelled to read the description?
4. And, if promoting your AFW online, is the title search-engine (i.e., Google search) friendly?

Below is a sample title that passes the four-prong test with flying colors!

Eliminate Unnecessary Costs That Are Reducing the Profitability of Your Small Business
Learn How to Restore the Financial Health of Your Company by Finding and Purging These Painful Expenses

There are two title pitfalls to avoid when naming your AFW. As shared earlier, using your book title as the title of your AFW is a recipe for failure because it conveys breadth, not depth. Another related pitfall is the use of numbers in the title. If your title presents 10 ways to do such and such, you run the same risk of conveying a broad message. Since the webinar duration is limited, your prospects desire depth. Few will believe you can provide depth into 10 elements in one hour.

Paragraph 1 – The Issue

When you developed the scope of your AFW, you identified the problem you will solve for buyers and attendees and the impact of inaction. The first paragraph of your AFW description, called *The Issue*, presents the problem and the ramifications of not solving that problem now. This paragraph is the sales parallel of conducting a needs analysis discussion with your prospect. Unfortunately, you cannot have a two-way interaction with a reader. So, this paragraph has to communicate what you understand as the problem and present it to the reader.

This paragraph creates a vivid picture in the mind of your prospective registrants of pain they are experiencing and the ramification of not resolving that issue now.

The *Issue* paragraph includes three sentences: *Hook, Challenge,* and *Impact.*

The *Hook* begins the AFW description and is designed to quickly grab the reader. There are four types of effective hooks.

1. **A compelling statistic related to the problem you solve.**

    84% of companies struggle with profitability.

2. **A quote based on what your target buyer might be saying about this problem.**

    "Why aren't my sales people hitting their numbers?"

3. **An engaging statement.**

    Most business owners consider the economic downturn to be a threat to their survival, but savvy entrepreneurs embrace it as a tremendous opportunity.

4. **A non-rhetorical question.**

    Starting an AFW description with "Would you like to have more profits?" has the potential to irritate some prospects. After all, why would they want fewer profits? Yet, a question can be a great way to grab your reader, make them think and lead them to the next part of your webinar description.

What is your plan to increase profits?

After the reader has been "hooked," the *Challenge* sentence presents the problem that is plaguing the target buyer of your AFW, not the prospective attendee. You want to engage the people holding the checkbook to motivate them to purchase your AFW. Hold their interest by succinctly describing the problem that your AFW will be addressing. Push their emotional hot buttons relative to this problem. Are they frustrated? Scared? Annoyed? Threatened? The better able you are to arouse emotion, the more eager your prospects will be to find a resolution to their problems.

While increasing revenue may help, you need to find the unnecessary, hidden costs that are sucking the profits out of your firm.

With the challenge presented, the next step is to reveal the ramifications of not addressing the problem now -- the *Impact* sentence. We all have problems, but we aren't trying to tackle them all today. Help your prospects understand why they have to take action now. This is a key element of the description and is the driver of action! If there isn't a motivation to solve the problem, you will have webinar description readers, but not buyers.

If you can't locate these costs, it's impossible to address them which leaves your bottom-line ... not to mention your entire business ... at risk.

To be effective, this *Issue* paragraph must leave prospects feeling that it is both *important* and *urgent* to solve the problem. If you're missing either of these ingredients, prospects will not be highly motivated to register for your event. Instead, your AFW will be something they might consider – but quite possibly forget. Guide prospects so they understand that they need your training right now.

Paragraph 2 – The Solution

Now your prospect is acutely aware of the issue that is plaguing them and the result of inaction. The task is to make them feel better. The *Solution* paragraph positions you as the expert who has solved this issue for countless others over the years. This isn't the place to solve the problem, but rather where you position yourself as someone who can solve the problem.

Imagine you were in dire need of medical attention. Would you care how the doctor solves your problem? Of course, you wouldn't. You would care about her expertise and experience in solving the problem for others. That is your goal with this paragraph, to position your prowess in solving this problem.

The *Solution* paragraph also has three components: *Credibility, Descriptor,* and *Synergy.*

The first sentence presents your two most relevant credentials, which is why this sentence is referred to as *Credibility.* You wrote those down when you responded to this question in Chapter 4: "Why should I learn how to solve this problem from you?"

Here is an easy formula to develop your *Credibility* sentence.

1. Your name
2. Your two most relevant and powerful credentials
3. Conclude with "helps <insert your audience> <describe the challenge you help your clients overcome>."

> *John Smith, author of "Big and Little" and management thought leader, helps business leaders find the costs that are destroying their profitability.*

The second sentence, the *Descriptor,* expands upon your credibility and shares what you will teach in the webinar.

> *He teaches you how to find the rocks that are hiding the expenses that weigh down your business.*

The third and final sentence, the *Synergy,* connects the solution with the problem. Read the *Impact* sentence from the *Issue* paragraph for clues, as this sentence should synergize the problem with the solution. It should instill confidence that participation in this virtual training course will help solve this problem.

Paint the big picture for your prospects! Illustrate will be delivered in the training – and more importantly, the major benefits prospects will get by attending. Pick the most relevant benefit with the greatest impact so that prospects can see how they will be enriched through your teachings.

Below are some of the proven *Synergy* winners with AFWs:

- Increased profits
- Increased revenue
- Shorter sales cycle
- Better qualified prospects
- Reduced employee turnover
- Increased market share
- Greater efficiency and productivity
- Decreased risk
- Increased marketing response rates
- Decreased costs

> *Discover the important areas you should research - and questions you should ask of your management team - to drive the profitability of your company.*

Bullet Points – The Takeaways

When creating this bulleted list of *Takeaways*, you want to manage the number of bullets you use. Too few bullets, and prospects won't get a sense of what you'll be teaching or, worse yet, won't think that you're delivering enough value for the registration fee. Too many bullets points, however, and they won't believe you can adequately cover the material in the amount of time you have allotted for your AFW.

The next section of a compelling AFW description presents the *Takeaways* prospects will gain by participating in your training. The *Takeaways* are the bullet points of the AFW description and list the skills that will be acquired in your virtual training. The attendees spend an hour with you and come away being able to do what? What will they be able to do, or do better, immediately following your virtual training?

As you were preparing to write your AFW description, what was your response to "What skills will be acquired in the virtual training session?" This is the content for the five bullet points that comprise the *Takeaways* portion of your AFW description. Think of this like a game show. Fill in the following blank: "In this webinar, you will learn how to _____."

> *Visit StopSpeakingForFree.com for bullet point starters and enter AFW4ME.*

Oftentimes, prospects will read the Takeaways before reading the remainder of your webinar description. The Takeaways should provide in detail how you solve the presented issue. Write one statement for each major concept you'll be presenting in your webinar. As a general rule, develop five strong bullet points for your one-hour AFW. Here is a four-step process to develop each of your Takeaways:

1. **List the skills to be acquired beginning with** *"You will learn how to:"* **Repeat this process for each of your five Takeaways.**

2. **Add more color and description.** The more descriptive you are, the better your chances of getting prospects to connect with you and your webinar.

   You will learn how to:

   • *Find the costly, unnecessary expenses*

3. **Highlight the benefits.** This step makes your description more compelling by spelling out the benefits your prospects will gain when they master the lessons you will teach. To help flesh out your content, review your list of concepts and ask yourself "So what?" after each point. Keep asking the question until you've identified the benefit of each lesson and what it means to the prospects.

   You will learn how to:

   • *Find the costly, unnecessary expenses that are killing your business ... so you can eliminate each one*

4. **Tease.** Want to spice up your copy even more? Add a bit of intrigue to your marketing by teasing your readers, making them extremely curious about what you'll be teaching. Incorporating specifics, such as the number of steps in a process or the number of methods you will teach, is a great way to increase curiosity. (However, be aware that some prospects may view your copy as unbelievable if every bullet point includes quantities. Just like the title consideration, you want to make sure that the reader doesn't think that it is impossible to provide depth on the topic in a short session.)

   You will learn how to:

   • *Find the costly, unnecessary expenses that are killing your business... so you can eliminate each one using a three-step analytical process*

The Giveaway

The *Giveaway* section immediately follows the bullet points. This is your opportunity to provide additional value to the attendees. Remember, giveaways or bonuses are a great way to add value to your event. If you select a giveaway, such as an eBook or white paper, that further demonstrates your mastery of the subject matter being taught in your webinar, it also serves as a tangible reminder of your expertise. The *Giveaway* should not be something that is readily offered for free (i.e., an article).

To add even more impact, tell prospective attendees how much the *Giveaway* is worth. To maintain credibility, use a price that prospects would reasonably expect to pay if purchasing the *Giveaway*. If the value assigned is too high – such as $97 dollars for a four-page "report" – you will lose credibility, as well as fail to position your AFW as an educational event.

You can also use the *Giveaway* section as a motivator to buy now. If you limit the quantity of what you are giving away, it could get your prospects to pull out their credit card today.

As an added bonus, the first 50 registrants receive John's white paper, "Profitability Management for Business Leaders" to help you implement the teachings from this eLearning training course.

Sample AFW Description

In this chapter, we've been building a webinar description. Below is a sample based on what was constructed using the aforementioned methodology.

**Eliminate Unnecessary Costs That Are
Reducing the Profitability of Your Small Business**
Learn How to Restore the Financial Health
of Your Company by Finding and Purging
These Painful Expenses

What is your plan to increase profits? While increasing revenue may help, you need to find the unnecessary, hidden costs that are sucking the profits out of your firm. If you can't locate these costs, it's impossible to address them ... which leaves your bottom-line - not to mention your entire business - at risk.

John Smith, author of "Big and Little" and management

thought leader, helps business leaders find the costs that are destroying their profitability. He teaches you how to find the rocks that are hiding the expenses that weigh down your business. Discover the important areas you should research, and questions you should ask of your management team, to drive the profitability of your company.

In this webinar, you'll learn how to:

- Find the costly, unnecessary expenses that are killing your business ... so you can eliminate each one using a three-step analytical process
- Review each expense to determine its validity and necessity to the business
- Engage your management time to solicit their input on cost reduction strategies
- Create a cost-conscious culture among your employees to improve profitability
- Develop programs to reward those who are most effective at improving the corporate bottom-line

As an added bonus, the first 50 registrants receive John's white paper, "Profitability Management for Business Leaders," to help you implement the teachings from this eLearning training course.

Putting This Methodology into Practice

The chapter began by telling you that the AFW Description Copywriting Methodology is presented in a logical fashion. The order in which the information is presented is not the way to develop your copy. Below is the recommended order when crafting your AFW description:

1. Takeaways – five bullet points
2. Close – Giveaway

3. Solution – Credibility
4. Solution – Descriptor
5. Issue – Hook
6. Issue – Challenge
7. Issue – Impact
8. Solution – Synergy
9. Title
10. Subtitle

Here is why the process is structured in this fashion.

- The *Takeaways* section is relatively easy to complete and defines the scope of the AFW.

- The *Giveaway* section is also very straightforward.

- The *Solution – Credibility/Descriptor* come to mind easily after developing your *Takeaways*.

- The *Solution – Synergy* is saved until later because you can't write it without fleshing out the *Issue* section, particularly *Issue – Impact*.

- The *Title* and *Subtitle* are the last steps because, as you write the AFW description, naming ideas will reveal themselves.

Once your AFW description is written, get feedback from colleagues to ensure the message is clear and compelling. If you're fortunate enough to have members of your prospective audience review your webinar description, ask if they understand the value of participating and whether they agree it would be a good investment. If you get anything but a resounding "yes," keep tweaking your copy until it's clear and irresistible.

Other Registrant Conversion Tools

Congratulations! You've written an AFW description that provides an accurate and compelling presentation of what attendees will learn and how they will benefit from participating in your webinar. In addition to the AFW description, consider incorporating these other tools as part of the registrant conversion process. These additional elements might appear as sidebars on a web page, on additional pages on your web site, or as additional sections on your web page or in printed promotions.

Summary Speaker Bio

In the AFW description, you highlighted your key credentials. However, you may want to have a one- or two-paragraph summarized bio presented as a narrative on your webinar marketing materials. You can use this tool to further reinforce why you are the thought leader from whom prospective participants should learn this content.

Start off with a sentence that accurately summarizes your expertise with the subject matter. Then, flesh out your bio with more details about how you gained your expertise including:

- Education, training and certifications

- Association memberships

- Current and past jobs (if they are relevant)

- Clients and industries as they relate to the subject matter

- Books, audio programs and other educational materials you've created

- Volunteer opportunities and positions held

- Awards and commendations earned

What should not be included ... information that does not support your argument that you are a well-qualified, if not the best, instructor for the eLearning event. In general, you don't need to share personal details such as where you live, how many children or grandchildren you have, to whom you are married, what your hobbies are, or how long you've lived in a certain area. The only time these facts should be included would be if they pertain to your topic. For example, it's appropriate to discuss your family if you are teaching a parenting-related webinar or otherwise need to show that you relate to parents.

Testimonials

Earlier, you learned that the most effective testimonials are specific, concise, and relevant to the webinar topic. Testimonials are critical to the AFW registrant conversion process because they demonstrate the experience others have had with you. Don't limit your scope to comments from people who have been through this webinar before. Also, use testimonials from those who have experienced you on this subject matter in other ways such as a consultant, trainer, or keynote speaker.

If you are offering a new AFW and don't yet have testimonials specific to this event, use testimonials from other trainings you've delivered. Alternatively, present testimonials about your mastery of the subject matter, for example, testimonials from consulting clients or from an in-person event you delivered on the topic.

6 Developing Your Webinar Marketing Plan

Implement Creative Strategies to Reach Prospective Registrants at the Right Time

With your AFW description in hand, you are ready to promote. This chapter focuses on the development of a campaign to generate registrations. There are two important points from earlier chapters to keep in mind as you work through this material:

1. The bulk of your registrations will come in **during the last 48 hours before your AFW**, so your strongest marketing push should be during the last week before your event. The primary benefit of promotional activities before this time will be to raise awareness of your AFW.

2. The conversion process for *Fans*, *Acquaintances*, and *Strangers* is vastly different and you need to be sensitive to the conversion drivers for each of them.

Lay the Foundation

The first step when promoting an AFW is to determine what your primary marketing tool will be. In 99.9% of cases, this will be a web page that you will use to attract interested prospects. The web page may be on your web site or, if your AFW is being promoted by a training company as part of its lineup of eLearning events, on a provider's website.

> *Visit StopSpeakingForFree.com to view a sample webinar promotional page. Enter AFW4ME.*

Once your AFW promotion page is in place, now you are ready to drive visibility to your virtual training event ... and generate registrations. Following is a suggested promotional schedule.

4 Weeks Out

Identify and Contact Potential Affiliates (*Acquaintances*)

Potential affiliates (individuals and organizations who promote your AFW for a commission) include other speakers, trainers, consultants and experts who work with your target audience. Another great resource is associations whose members are your ideal attendees – especially those organizations with whom you already have a connection. Remember, these are members of the *Acquaintance* group that you want to leverage.

Add Mention of Your AFW to Your Email Signature

Each day, you send dozens of emails. Why not leverage this contact point by reminding clients and prospects that you offer an eLearning training program? Writing a short description of your upcoming AFW takes just a few minutes. Be sure to include a link to the web page that describes your AFW in full detail. Rather than show just the hyper-link to the AFW Description web page, show the title along with a hyper-link to the AFW description page.

Update Your Training Schedule

Do you have your AFW schedule on your website? If so, make sure your webinar is listed, along with a hyper-link to your AFW description page. This is another great way to keep clients and prospective clients apprised of your offering. Posting a notice of your event on your home page is also a great way to announce your news. If you've scheduled several AFWs, you may want to add a calendar page to your site to feature all of your upcoming events.

2-3 Weeks Out

Publish articles

One of the best ways to drive visibility to your AFWs is by writing and publishing articles. Article marketing is a proven strategy for increasing traffic to your website. People who are actively seeking solutions to their challenges go to the Internet to find answers. Search engines love well-written articles and will offer up your written advice to people searching online for answers. Select topics that are related to your AFWs and write 600- to 800-word articles that compel the reader to pay attention to this issue or opportunity. Articles can be included in your e-zine for distribution to your *Fans*. Publish the articles on websites throughout the Internet, in your blog, as well as on your own website.

As you write the article, be mindful of search engine optimization and search engine marketing keywords to help the search engines find your articles. Conclude the article with a mention of your upcoming virtual training event, and create a hyperlink to the AFW description page. You may want to consider offering an incentive, such as a 10% discount, if registrants mention the article when they enroll.

Articles give you the opportunity to demonstrate expertise and experience to prospective registrants, particularly those who are not familiar with you. Want to get their names in your database? In the article, include an offer for a free tip sheet and have them email you to request a copy. When they request the tip sheet, add them to your database list.

> *For a list of 100 websites where you can publish your articles for free, visit StopSpeakingForFree.com and enter AFW4ME.*

Event Directories

Many publications and web sites include directories of upcoming events. Providing such information helps secure their position as a source of relevant, timely news. As such, many calendars offer free listings, as long as your AFW topic will appeal to the publication's or site's readers.

> *For a list of directories where you can*
> *list AFWs, visit*
> *StopSpeakingForFree.com and enter AFW4ME.*

When listing your AFW, you will include basic event details, such as date/time, fees, where to learn more, and how to register. Also include as much of your AFW description as you can. Most event calendars limit the number of words that you can use to describe your content. At a minimum, try to include one sentence from the *Issue* paragraph, another from the *Solution*, and a third sentence to list three *Takeaways*.

Save the Date Email

Remember, any marketing done this far in advance serves primarily to raise awareness of your topic and event. Why not send a short email to your *Fans*, asking them to reserve the date on their calendar for your AFW? Include a brief description of what you'll teach, and be sure to include the date and time.

The Last 7 Days

Social Media

Social media tools such as LinkedIn®, Twitter®, and Facebook® provide an easy way to report about the progress you're making. You can send out updates announcing that webinar registration is open or reminding prospects of the major benefits of attending your training. You can also send out updates about the latest developments, such as doing a run-through, finishing your PowerPoint®

slides, or registration levels. At the time of this book's printing, LinkedIn® is the primary social media tool for promoting AFWs that are business-related. In Chapter 7, you will read more about leveraging LinkedIn® to drive attendance.

Email Promotions

In the last seven days before your AFW, it's time to switch into heavy promotion mode. Plan to contact your list at least three times via email with the sole purpose of inviting them to register for your AFW. At least one of your contacts should be in the last two days before your event. The easiest and most effective approach is to guide prospects to the promotional page on your website.

Another approach is to send mini-sales letters via email. This type of message will contain all of the information presented in your AFW description, but the message will be more personal and less rigidly structured. Be sure to include the key information from your AFW description.

> *Visit StopSpeakingForFree.com and enter*
> *AFW4ME to view a sample email promotion.*

Overcome Your Marketing Reluctance

If you are like many speakers, you may be hesitant to send multiple email messages that are promotional in nature. Your wariness is understandable – after all, subscribers typically join a list to receive information and valuable resources, not promotional messages.

However, emails that focus solely on promoting your AFW, rather than mentioning your event in passing – play a strategic role in selling seats. Prospects are bombarded by marketing messages. If you want to stand out from the crowd, you need to keep your name and event in front of your prospects. The squeaky wheel gets oiled – and the persistent marketer gets the registrations.

Rather than feeling guilty and anxious about "bothering" your *Fans*, focus on how prospects will benefit once they participate.

Remember, you are making them aware of a training event that will help them overcome a problem – not delivering an obnoxious infomercial. Envisioning how your prospects will benefit from attending your event, rather than how you will benefit by filling your event, can help you reframe the act of contacting your *Fans* one more time as a service, rather than a nuisance. By doing all you can to make them aware of this valuable training, you're doing your prospects a favor.

If you're truly uncomfortable sending multiple promotional messages, try one of the following:

- **Make your last message, delivered the day before or the day of your AFW, a short courtesy reminder about the event.** Your email should provide the basics about your event and a link to the web page where prospects can learn more. The key message is that it is the last chance to participate.

- **Incorporate helpful content into your promotional messages.** You could share a tip (related to the topic about which you'll be speaking, of course) and then tell your readers that you'll be sharing more about the topic in your webinar. Then segue into providing more information about the event.

Because they require a much smaller commitment of time – as well as money – selling seats in AFWs typically is easier than promoting in-person events. But that doesn't mean that you can send out a single promotion and fill all of your virtual seats. Start early to raise awareness, especially among people who don't know you or your company. Then continue promoting right up to the start time of your AFW to ensure that your marketing message is in front of prospects when they are ready to buy – the crucial 48 hours before your event.

7 | Using LinkedIn® to Generate Webinar Registrations

Leverage the Power of Social Media and Networking to Expand Your Marketing Reach

It wasn't long ago that the success of your events was dependent on your ability to effectively use email marketing to reach your *Fans*. If you wanted to reach *Strangers*, you had to be prepared to invest significant dollars in your event marketing campaign. With the explosion of social media, however, you now have the ability to reach thousands of prospective registrants without spending a nickel to do it. Social media has become one of the most widespread and fast-growing marketing tools.

To effectively use social marketing to promote attendee-funded webinars (AFWs), you need a marketing strategy. Many speakers think that "social marketing" means entering your URL into LinkedIn® and other social media platforms, then kicking back and watching registrants come in droves. Alas, anyone who has tried that strategy has found it to be a failure.

To reach your target audience through social media, select your campaign's primary platform. Two of the largest players are Facebook® andLinkedIn®. However, they are not competitors in the traditional sense of the word. These two social networking platforms have two very different audiences. LinkedIn® has become the leader in business networking while Facebook® is recognized for social communication. For example, it is rare that someone shares family information onLinkedIn®, and Facebook® members are often angered by the promotion of business-related functions.

When promoting AFWs that deliver business training, your best investment of time is LinkedIn®, which offers a number of opportunities to reach potential registrants. (Note: Although the focus of this chapter is LinkedIn®, the concepts are applicable with other social media platforms, as well.) Here are the key elements to consider when using LinkedIn®.

Your Bio

As a LinkedIn® member, you are provided with a profile page, the core of which is your bio. Although your entire profile page can be used to build your credibility, prospective registrants begin their evaluation of your AFW by focusing first on the presenter's bio.

When prospective registrants comes across your AFW on LinkedIn® and are interested in learning more, they immediately visit your LinkedIn® profile. They evaluate your expertise on the subject matter you are teaching with two questions in mind: "Why should I learn from you? What makes you a leading expert on this subject?"

One of the biggest challenges when developing a LinkedIn® bio is that you likely have multiple areas of expertise. This makes it challenging to weave a coherent story for your bio. Instead, your bio becomes an information buffet with no clear message. To quickly attract your target audience, your bio must clearly position your expertise for the business prospects you desire. If it doesn't, you will not be successful generating registrants through this medium.

For example, LinkedIn® does not require that you provide your entire employment history. Since you are not using this platform to search for a job, provide only the information that supports your marketing message. It may be that the only entry you have is the consulting firm you founded five years ago. That's perfectly fine. However, you may also have 20 years of related experience working for others. In that case, you should consider including that information as it further supports your expertise. Think of this as the marketing portion of the site. You have total control over what you provide -- or don't provide.

In addition to your written bio, you have the opportunity to share your photo. This is a good idea, as photos help to form a connection with your potential attendees. Give careful consideration to the photo that you select for your profile page. If you want people to take you seriously as an expert, make sure your photo looks professional. Don't use a personal webcam picture; spend the $100 to get a professional business photo taken, if you don't already have one. Consider this: if you haven't made the small financial investment to get a professional photo taken, what message are you conveying to those who might buy your AFW? How can you argue that your webinar is worth a financial investment to attend if you won't make a similar investment to promote it?

Recommendations

A synonym for recommendations is references or testimonials. One of the most powerful conversion tools for AFWs is testimonials from those who have experienced your teachings on the subject matter you will be presenting. However, an endless listing of generic testimonials saying how great you are will not get the job done.

Put yourself in the prospect's seat for a moment. If you were considering investing in an AFW, what would be the most critical due diligence step? You would want to hear from others how great the presenter is, right? But you would want specifics. You would look for comments about what information was taught, why it was beneficial, and the results that the attendee received from putting the teachings into practice. Here is an example of an effective recommendation:

> *I had the opportunity to participate in John's webinar on building a client database and found the session to be tremendously informative. John presented a number of strategies and techniques that I was able to quickly put into practice. I was able to triple the size of my database in four weeks. He made learning online fun and engaging ... I look forward to taking more courses with him.*

-Bill Wilson, Executive Director, ABC Foundation

What made this an effective recommendation? First, the recommendation was very specific about the course that was taken. It summarized what was learned. Most importantly, it provided the results that the attendee experienced by participating in the session. In essence, it has everything you would be looking for when evaluating a speaker and her virtual training event on LinkedIn®.

Leverage Groups

One of the great benefits of social media platforms is the groups function. At the time of this printing, LinkedIn® allows you to join up to 50 groups as a free member. Joining is very easy: You click a "request to join" link and await the group owner's approval. To see noticeable results, however, do not join just any group. You need to have a sophisticated approach to how you will participate.

The first step is to join groups whose members fit your profile of the ideal AFW buyer. For example, if you are delivering an AFW for small business owners, join groups that have small business owners as members. To find the right group, start by clicking "Groups" in the left-hand navigation panel. Once you are on the Groups page, use the "search groups" function (located at the top right of the web page) to enter keywords that relate to your target audience and/or area of expertise. The search will provide you with a list of groups, organized by size with the largest ones showing first. Fifty groups may seem like a lot, but you will be surprised how quickly you use your group membership options.

Your first temptation may be to join the largest groups that are presented. After all, that way you'll connect with a large number of potential prospects, right? No! The flaw in this approach is that the larger the group, the more quickly you will get lost in the crowd. With 25,000 members in a group, it is impossible to create an impact. Ideally, join groups that have between 1,000 and 5,000 members. At that size, the group has enough mass to justify your time investment, but is not so large that you are invisible.

Once you have joined a group, you may be eager to jump in by creating a discussion to tell the group about your upcoming AFW and that they should attend. Beware: if you do this, the group will blast you! First, a group's discussion area is considered sacred ground that must not be contaminated with blatant promotions. If you create a discussion to promote anything you do, you will be chastised – and perhaps even removed from the group. Typically, new LinkedIn® members make this mistake once – and only once. If you want to alert your groups about your upcoming AFWs, it is far more acceptable to use a group's news function to link to your AFW description page.

The news section is most often used for articles and is an excellent place to publish articles you have written on your area of expertise. It is also a great place to promote your upcoming AFW.

The news section is populated by copying and pasting a link to a newsworthy item. To create a new entry, enter a URL to a web page that describes your AFW. Then you will be asked to enter the title, brief description, and source of the news. After submitting the item, the entry appears in the group's news section, where it is available for viewing and comment. Since you now know when people buy AFW seats, wait until the week of the webinar to create a news item announcing your event. Another faux pas made in LinkedIn® groups is adding an entry in the news section more than once. Again, it's another way to get blasted.

Although the news section is the best place for direct promotion of your AFWs, it doesn't mean that the discussion section should be ignored. There is a tremendous opportunity to creatively use discussions to send prospective attendees your way. Remember, the big-picture reason to join a group is to position yourself as an expert, a thought leader, with your target audience. What's the best way to do that? Participate in discussions related to your expertise. The more frequently you contribute your knowledge and more wisdom you share, the more people will sit up and take notice of you.

> Since LinkedIn® does not have a spell- or grammar-check function, compose your responses in Microsoft Word® and proof them there. Then copy and paste your responses into LinkedIn®.

Another strategy is to create discussions that position you as an expert. If you are a member of a sales management group and are teaching an AFW about designing sales compensation programs, create a discussion that asks the group to share their philosophy on sales compensation. When group members respond to your discussion, you can do two things: invite them to join your network, and invite them to your AFW.

By contributing to and starting discussions, you will impress your target audience and intrigue them with your philosophy. Guess what they do when that happens? They click your name and visit your profile page to learn more about you. Now, you can see why your bio, photo and recommendations are so important.

Another component of your social media strategy may be the creation of your own group, which is very easy to do as a free member on LinkedIn®. While setting up the group is easy, it is much more challenging to get your target audience to join and return frequently. Remember, they can only join 50 groups too, so your target audience will be choosey about which groups they join. They must believe that participating in your group will enrich their lives with valuable content and connections; otherwise, joining will not be worth their time. To make it easier to launch and grow a robust group, start by participating in other groups. This will enable you to develop a following. Before creating a group, make sure that you are committed to active leadership. Creating a group solely to drive attendance to your AFWs is not the best use of your time.

Building Your Network

The social media phenomenon means that you need to be focused on building a new distribution list – your social media network – beyond your *Fans*. In LinkedIn®, your social media network consists of your "connections" – the people to whom you are linked.

There are two general ways to approach this: go on a mission of mass (i.e., build a large network) or have a commitment to quality. Some LinkedIn® users are on a crusade to build the biggest LinkedIn® network. These individuals are usually identified as LION, which stands for LinkedIn® Open Networker. They don't care much about who is in their network; they want quantity. But if your goal is to drive registrations in AFWs, you should focus on *quality* connections, not *quantity*.

Networks are essential to success in social marketing because they enable you to communicate directly to qualified prospects. In LinkedIn®, the people in your network see the updates you enter in your profile. They see when you are active in groups. In addition, you can email them directly within LinkedIn® to share news of your webinar.

Let's revisit our earlier example of a sales compensation webinar being delivered by a sales management expert. The virtual presenter would want a network of professionals who are responsible for sales compensation, such as sales managers, vice presidents of sales, finance professionals, small business owners, and senior business executives. But how do you build your network?

It pays to be choosey when determining the types of individuals you will add to your network (as you do when joining groups). If you were the aforementioned sales management expert, you joined and became active in groups with the prospects listed above. As you become active in the groups, you earn the right to invite group members to your network.

Inviting someone to join your network is as easy as clicking a button – in the case of LinkedIn®, the button listed on the right side of all profile pages. When you click the "Add to your network" link, the system asks how you know this person and provides a text box with default language. Do not use the default language provided by LinkedIn®! Instead, take advantage of the text box to create a warm first impression with the person you are inviting to your network. Be sure to remind him/her how you are linked. It is important to note that you can get kicked out of LinkedIn® if you are inviting people with whom you have no relationship. If they respond to your invitation with "I don't know him/her," you will be penalized. If you get five of these negative marks in your file, you face sanctions, including having your network expansion suspended. People to consider inviting to your network include:

- Group owners of the groups you've joined

- Group managers of the groups you've joined

- Group members who have been involved in the same discussions in which you are participating

- Group members who have added comments to discussions you've created

- Group members who have added comments to news items you've created

Another reason to build your network is to leverage the "network updates" function, which allows any updates that you post to be shown in summary on your profile page immediately. In addition, unless you opt to turn this function off, LinkedIn® will send you a weekly email summarizing the updates that people in your network have shared. This allows you to keep tabs on what your network is doing, opening up countless opportunities to reconnect with and support the people with whom you are connected. In addition, remember that your updates also will be shared with your network. Use this function to share articles and, of course, to promote your upcoming AFW.

Another little secret about your LinkedIn® network. Did you know that you can export the contact information (including email addresses)? You can! Log-in to your account and click on "Contacts." Scroll down the bottom of the page and you will see a link titled "Export Connections." You can easily export your entire network to a .csv file, which can then be imported into the email system of your choosing. Be mindful of email best practices when communicating with these contacts.

Events Function

Once you have a robust network of your target prospective attendees, you can leverage LinkedIn®'s event listing section. In the left-hand column of your LinkedIn® home page, select "events." In the top navigation pane, select "Add an Event." Enter all of the information about your upcoming AFW. Once done, as a free member, you can invite 50 people from your network to your event using this feature. They will receive an email with the event information.

Although email marketing to your opt-in database is a tried-and-true way to promote AFWs, relying primarily on this tool is risky. Hypervigiliant spam filters frequently intercept legitimate email, making it impossible to guarantee that prospects will receive your messages. In addition, busy professionals are bombarded with email each day, making it difficult to break through the inbox clutter. Social media marketing is an easy and increasingly popular way to stay in front of your audience and keep them updated about your webinars. Using the steps outlined in this chapter will not only help drive registrants, but will also help to build your brand in the marketplace.

8 | Getting Media Attention for Your Virtual Training Events

Promote Your Attendee-Funded Webinars for Pennies

by Dan Janal

Leveraging the media is another great way to reach a wider audience with a relatively small investment of time and money. Here are proven steps for using the media to reach prospects far beyond your *Fans*, build your list, and promote your attendee-funded webinars (AFWs).

1. Write a Press Release

The media are constantly searching for news items to cover. Press releases are the standard method for communicating story ideas to the reporters who cover your topic. Many trade publications, online and print publication, publish notices about upcoming events. To secure a spot on these calendars, submit a press release that contains the particulars of your AFW:

- The title of your AFW
- Date and time (be sure to include time zones)
- The price of the webinar
- What topics will be discussed
- Who the appropriate audience is (perhaps by skill level, i.e., beginner, intermediate or advanced)
- How to register. Be sure to list the web page on which you have

your AFW description, not your home page. Visitors who are directed to the front page of your web site may not find your webinar registration page

- Contact information, including your phone number, email and website

Keys To Writing An Effective AFW Press Release

1. The headline of the press release should:
   - include the words *virtual training* or *webinar*
   - list at least one target audience
   - reference the major benefit for the target audience

2. The first paragraph, similar to your AFW description, positions the problem you are solving (The *Issue*) and ramifications of not addressing that issue now. This paragraph should be one to two sentences.

3. The second paragraph presents the AFW information.
   - Open with how the virtual training helps the defined audience
   - Include: date, day, time, registration fee, and link to the AFW description page

4. The third paragraph positions your expertise relative to the subject you are teaching (The *Solution*).

5. Present the skills that are going to be acquired in your webinar (*Takeaways*).

6. If you are including a bonus (*Giveaway*) with the registration, share that next.

7. Present your summary bio.

Sample Press Release

For Immediate Release

Contact:

John Smith
Big and Little Management Consultants
media@bigandlittlemanagementconsultants.com
615-555-1212
bigandlittlemanagementconsultants.com

New Virtual Training Teaches Small-Business Owners and Executives How to Find and Eliminate Unnecessary Costs that Reduce Business Profitability

Anytown, MN– March 1, XXXX – Increasing revenue may improve the profitability of your business. But to maximize profitability, you also need to find the unnecessary, hidden costs that are sucking the profits out of your firm. If you can't locate these costs, it's impossible to address them, which leaves your bottom-line – not to mention your entire business – at risk.

A new virtual training event will help small-business owners and executives find and eliminate unnecessary expenses. The webinar will be held 3 p.m. Eastern, Wednesday, April 14, XXXX. The fee for attending is $99 per connection. To register, go to www.abcmanagementexperts.com/webinar.

The online session will be delivered by John Smith, author of "Big and Little" and management thought leader. A consultant with 25 years of experience helping thousands of business owners eradicate unnecessary expenses, John is the master of getting inside the true financial workings of a company to ensure profitability. Discover the important areas you should research – and questions you should ask of your management team – to drive the profitability of your company.

You will learn how to:

- Find the costly, unnecessary expenses that are killing your business and eliminate each one using a 3-step analytical process
- Review each expense to determine its validity and necessity to the business

- Engage your management time to solicit their input on cost reduction strategies
- Create a cost-conscious culture among your employees to improve profitability
- Develop programs to reward those who are most effective at improving the corporate bottom-line

As a bonus, you will receive a copy of Smith's white paper, "Profitability Management for Business Leaders."

About John Smith

John Smith has helped more than 5,000 small businesses increase their profitability in the last decade. In addition to 25 years of management consulting experience, Smith spent 10 years as an executive manager in two Fortune 100 companies. Author of "Big and Little," Smith is an adjunct professor of business management at the Minnesota School of Business Management.

2. Distribute Your Press Release

About a month before your AFW, send an email to online publications and blogs. When targeting print publications, email your press release to reporters about four months before the event. But this is not all you can – or should – do to distribute your press release.

One of the most overlooked benefits of publicity is the fact that Google likes PR and will rate your website higher if you have links from the media. Although it's wonderful for prospects to see your press releases, it's just as important for Google to find them. As Google indexes your press releases (i.e., adds the pages on which your press releases are posted to its index of web pages to which it directs search engine users), your search engine ranking will improve. Then, when prospects are searching Google to find a company or consultant just like you, your site will appear near the top of the search results.

But let's face it, not all links are created equal. A link from my site to yours is nice. A link from someone else's blog to your site is even better. But a link from *The New York Times* is top notch in

Google's eyes. So it is important to post your press releases online. Press releases can be posted on:

- Your website, where the search engines will eventually index the page – on their own time schedule. Also use Facebook®, LinkedIn® and Twitter® to drive traffic to these pages, just as you learned to do with articles and your AFW descriptions earlier in this book.

- Paid press release distribution sites like PR WEB, PR Newswire, Business Wire and ExpertClick.com. All of these services have relationships with Google to index their clients' press releases – that is, to add the web page on which the press release appears to Google's index. Although there is no guarantee that your press releases will be indexed, unless you cross an ethical or moral line, the chances are pretty good that your press releases will appear in Google within 48 hours.

Beware of "free" press release distribution sites. Most reviews I've read about them show that they have no reach – or they are "fronts" for services that try to get you to pay.

To fully capitalize on the power of publicity, don't stop your media relations work once your webinar has been delivered. Use the next four tips to fully leverage your AFW's publicity opportunities to further position yourself as an expert, reach prospective attendees for future events, and sell recordings of your past AFWs.

3. Take Advantage of "People in the Business" Columns

The fact that you delivered a virtual training event is news. Every local newspaper has a "People in Business" column that runs once or twice a week. Trade and regional publications have similar sections. To be listed, send a short note to the editor of that section and tell them you delivered a training webinar. Because the listings in these types of columns are short, your announcements should be only one or two sentences long. For example:

Dan Janal, president of PR LEADS.com of Excelsior, MN, delivered a virtual training session hosted by Business Expert Webinars. He spoke about turning publicity into profits.

Be sure to list the webinar topic. Also, provide your contact information in case they have questions or need to confirm details with you.

> Send your picture. These columns usually run photos. Give them the opportunity to print yours!

If your city has a weekly business newspaper, send the announcement there, as well. If your state has a business magazine, send it there, too. As mentioned above, local papers love local news. Their mission is to get local people into print. Help them help you.

4. Position Yourself as the Expert to Reporters

Once you have spoken on a topic, many reporters consider you to be an expert on that topic. Take advantage of this fact by pitching reporters to write a story about your topic and feature you as the expert.

Note, I didn't say, "Write a story about you." No one cares about you, except your parents. Readers care about topics. So if you spoke about negotiating skills, you could suggest an article that:

- Provides a basic overview of the topic, such as the keys to successful negotiating.

- Ties it to a news event, such as how Democrats and Republicans in the Senate can improve their negotiating tactics.

- Includes an angle that touches the lives of normal people, such as how to negotiate for a pay raise at work or how to negotiate with your kids so they do their chores.

The list is endless once you think about the practical applications of your topic. Again, the concept of *urgent* and *important* applies here.

5. Tell the World You Were Quoted in the Media

If you are fortunate enough to get publicity in print or online, be sure to leverage the publicity by telling the world. Start by sending an email to your friends, colleagues, current clients, former clients and prospects with a subject line that broadcasts your news. For example:

Dan Janal quoted in USA TODAY!

Sharing your publicity victories is a great way to stay in touch with your audience and let them know that your business is thriving. Why is this important? Well, you never know when a prospect or former client might be in the market for your services, just as you never know if a current client is being courted by a competitor. Having big-name media linked to you means that your customers have no reason to jump ship.

Publicity is an essential component of a comprehensive and successful AFW marketing plan. Publicity helps you reach a wider audience of prospects for very little money. In addition, it boosts your credibility. People trust the media. When prospects see you and your webinar mentioned in the press, you benefit from the implied endorsement provided by the publication or media web site in which you were mentioned.

8 Steps to Generate Greater AFW Publicity

1. Write a press release announcing your event.
2. Send the press release to media and bloggers.
3. Distribute the press release via paid distribution services.
4. Post the press release on your website.
5. Post the link to the press release on LinkedIn® Groups,

Facebook® and/or Twitter®.

6. Write a "People in Business (PIB)" Entry.

7. Submit "PIB" entry to local, state and regional business publications.

8. Email your *Fans* when you appear in the media.

About the Author

Crowned "an Internet marketing expert" by the Los Angeles Times, *Dan Janal is an internationally recognized speaker, Internet marketer and author of six books that have been translated into six languages. He is the leading authority on turning publicity into profits. He coaches service professionals at PublicityLeadstoProfits.com. He is the Founder and President of PRLeads.com, which has helped literally thousands of service professionals get the publicity they need to establish credentials as thought leaders. He was on the public relations team that launched America Online and counts among his clients IBM and* The Reader's Digest. *He is currently launching FreePublicityTools.com to help professionals find the best do-it-yourself publicity and marketing tools on the Internet.*

9 | Selecting a Webinar Back-Office Company

Perform Due Diligence on Webinar Providers to Pick the Right One

Until now, we have focused on things that you must do to create a stellar attendee-funded webinar (AFW). This chapter focuses on the piece you cannot provide – the operations and technology. To determine which of the many webinar technology providers will make the best match for your company, start by determining the service, support, and technology you need.

In your search for a webinar provider, you will come across both webinar conferencing and webinar hosting companies. While these terms are often used as synonymously, they are not identical. In most instances, webinar conferencing companies provide meetings that use webinar technology. Their technology is designed for web meetings and product demos. Webinar hosting companies provide the services you need for training webinars. Their technology is much more robust and their capabilities are much broader. The tricky part for you is that webinar providers often interchange the two expressions so you are left to figure out into which bucket they actually fall. This chapter presents additional aspects to consider when evaluating webinar technology providers so you will select the right one.

Webinar Management Services

Registration

A basic, yet critical, requirement for any AFW is the registration process. Most webinar technology providers offer a means to facilitate registration, capturing and storing the contact information that you require from each participant. For your convenience, look for a system that can also send reminders to your registered participants to ensure they attend your AFW.

Because the technology partner you select will be representing your company, it's critical to analyze the registration process from the registrant's perspective. As part of your due diligence, go through the entire registration process yourself to ensure that the experience your registrants will have is one that you want associated with your brand. Be sure to ask about customization of the registration form and corresponding cost, if any.

Payment Processing

Since your attendees will pay for admission to the webinar, you need a means to process their credit card payment. If you don't have your own *shopping cart*, you may want to consider opening an account with a payment-processing service like PayPal. If you handle payment processing yourself, through PayPal or a similar provider, you will need a way to register attendees in the AFW after they have paid which may be burdensome.

A more streamlined option is to select a webinar technology provider that offers both registration and credit card processing. This increases the cost of what you'll pay for their services, but the additional expense is easily offset by the reduction in administrative work that otherwise would be needed for you to process payments yourself. Although many webinar technology providers offer registration services and webinar-delivery technology, few offer credit card processing services.

Unique PIN Codes

Since you will be offering webinars for which the participants pay to attend, you need to ensure that only those who pay access your webinar. One of your requirements when selecting a provider is to have a unique PIN (Personal Identification Number) for both the webinar and phone service for each participant. A unique PIN means that each participant receives his own code to access the event. If a second person attempts to use the same code, he will not be able to access the AFW. Not all webinar companies offer this, but as you can imagine, it is a critical requirement when delivering AFWs. Many technology providers offer one link to the webinar and phone service that anyone can use to access the event. This is a surefire way to have lots of people in your webinar, but few of them as paid participants.

Presentation Tools

Depending upon your presentation style, you may wish to embellish your presentation using webinar tools like online markers, pointers, etc. Most webinar providers offer a tool set for the speaker to use in the webinar. When analyzing the tools offered by the provider, be sure to check if the tools are the same for both uploaded presentations and desktop sharing. Some technology providers offer a robust tool set for uploaded presentations, but offer a very limited set when sharing a desktop. This is an important consideration if you plan to show an application, a video, or a website.

Recording Capability

Although AFWs provide a wonderful revenue opportunity, many speakers limit their earning capacity by delivering only live AFWs. To maximize your revenue, select a technology provider that offers recording capabilities. That way, you'll be able to turn your recorded webinar into a product – and a passive income stream.

Not all webinar providers can record the audio and slides together. Of those that can, some charge an additional fee for the service. Some providers offer only an audio recording; however, an audio-only recording is not as saleable as a recording that also includes the visual presentation. To maximize the appeal and sales of your recorded webinar product, select a technology provider that includes a Flash recording (a video of your presentation with audio - like a movie) of your webinar as part of the package.

Training for Speakers

Every webinar technology has its nuances, and during your session is the wrong time to find out that you don't know how to use every aspect of your provider's unique technology. Whether you have delivered webinars before or this is your first venture, it makes sense to invest time becoming intimately familiar with the functionality of your provider's technology.

To shorten your learning curve, look for a provider that offers training on how to use its technology. Some providers have recorded tutorials, while others conduct live one-on-one sessions for the presenter. Based on your webinar and technology comfort level, select a provider that positions you for success in the event. If you need more hand-holding, pick a provider that offers the personal touch.

Telephonic Needs

One of the major factors that affects webinar technology pricing is how you handle the audio portion of the webinar. Using a toll-free number is the most expensive way to go. It's much more economical for you to offer the webinar using a toll call – that is, having the registrants pay for the call. Although there was a time when long-distance charges were an important consideration, the vast majority of prospective registrants no longer consider this expense when deciding whether or not to participate in training. Attendees who dial in from work are usually not concerned about long-distance charges, as the fee will be paid by their employer. Most people dialing in from home are equally unconcerned about telephone charges, as the fixed price long-distance packages that are widely available make long-distance calls extremely affordable. If you offer toll-free calls when your attendees don't see value in it, you will be losing as much as $10.00 per registrant from your bottom line for a one-hour virtual training session.

An even more economical approach is to deliver the webinar audio over the Internet (also called VoIP which is the acronym for Voice over Internet Protocol) so that attendees can listen through their computer speakers. If you go this route, offer a telephonic solution too, so that participants who do not have speakers in their computers still can participate using their telephones. While economical, there is a risk to audio delivered this way. The attendee's connection speed will affect the audio delivery speed so there could be a time lag between when your voice is heard and the slide is presented. To head off complaints from dissatisfied participants who are listening to your audio via their computer speakers or dialing in via Skype (a a VoIP technology), inform the attendee that their bandwidth will affect the audio and offer a telephonic solution as well.

Also, remember that if you plan to verbally interact with attendees during your webinar, those who are listening using VoIP will not be able to verbally communicate with you in the discussion. VoIP does not enable participants to speak during the webinar.

Event Staffing

On the day of the webinar, most speakers want to concentrate on the delivery of their training, not fidget with event management issues. If this sounds like you, select a provider that will host the event for you, providing a staff person to welcome callers to the event and introduce you. The host also will record the webinar (if you opt to record it) and manage the time, letting you know when you're getting close to your end time. Finally, the host will moderate questions from the audience. Questions are typically submitted via the chat function in the technology. The moderator will gather the questions and forward them to you or, alternatively, ask them of you during a pre-arranged question-and-answer period.

These premium services come with a price tag, of course. If

you have an assistant or colleague who can host your webinars, it makes economic sense to go that route. If not, and you are concerned about managing the technical and administrative side of your webinar, select a provider that has an operator who can handle those functions for you.

Pricing Strategy

A final factor to evaluate when comparing webinar management services is pricing structure. Some providers charge a flat per-registrant fee (be sure to ask if you have to buy a seat as the presenter). Ideally, you'll select a provider that does not charge a minimum fee for each webinar.

On the other hand, some providers offer monthly subscription rates for a preset number of webinar seats per event, per month, or both. The per-seat price offered by these providers is typically less than you will pay if you select a per-registrant pricing package.

When you are first starting out, a per-registrant fee without an AFW minimum is the least-risky pricing structure. Once you've developed a track record and confidence that you'll be able to sell a certain number of seats at each event, switching to a monthly subscription plan typically makes the most financial sense. A monthly subscription also is beneficial if you plan to host AFWs regularly.

User Experience

In addition to webinar management, the other evaluation criterion when shopping for a webinar back-office provider is the user experience. The provider you select will become a part of your team ... an extension of your brand. The service they deliver can have a dramatic impact on how your company and AFWs are perceived by your attendees. Be sure to evaluate these factors from the attendee perspective:

Technology Requirements

Some webinar technology platforms require the user to download software to participate in the event. If this is true of the provider you are considering, be aware of the risks associated with required software downloads.

Although downloads are designed to be easy and uncomplicated, you need to accept that a portion of your audience will experience a problem, either because of user error or because of a technology snafu. If attendees who are not technologically-savvy experience problems, they may decide to cancel their registration rather than call the webinar technology provider's help desk for assistance getting the software to work properly.

Requiring attendees to download software may scare off even potential registrants who work for organizations that provide inhouse technology support. Many employers have grown tired of employees downloading software onto their work computers and calling their help desk for assistance. Allowing software downloads exposes the company's computer network to risk of security breaches and virus attacks, as some employees may download software from less-than-reputable providers. But even if a download is virus-free, providing technology support to employees drives costs through the roof. To address this issue, most companies have prohibited users from downloading or installing software on their office computers. If your registrants work for such organizations and cannot download the required software (which today is usually ActiveX) to participate, you will take the hit when they are disappointed in the webinar experience and demand a refund.

For this reason, focus on webinar providers that do not require the participants to download software. Some require the presenter to install the application, but the users need only to be able to access the Internet.

However, a software download-free experience is not without its pitfalls. If you elect to use a company that does not require the presenter or the participants to download software, you may find that you cannot use "build slides" (slide animation) in PowerPoint or that you cannot share your desktop with the participants to show them a website or application. This results in a less dynamic and captivating presentation. If you elect to use a provider that requires a software download, ask for references from other presenters who have used the platform. Be sure to follow up with other users and inquire about their experiences with this aspect.

Another consideration related to technology is compatibility. Three areas to consider:

1. Does their platform work for both a PC and Mac?

Not all webinar platforms deliver a great user experience for both PC and Mac users.

2. What version of PowerPoint® does it support?

Finding out what version of PowerPoint® the technology supports is extremely important to you as the presenter, as it tells you what software to use for the visual portion of the webinar. Imagine finding out on the day of your event that the provider supports an earlier version of the software, not the one you spent countless hours preparing for your webinar.

3. What web browsers are compatible with their technology?

Not all webinar technologies work with all web browsers or all versions of them.

Polling

When delivering your AFW, an exciting way to engage the audience is to ask questions and have the audience respond with a virtual show of hands, which is done through polling. Polling allows you to ask the group multiple-choice or yes/no questions and have them respond online by clicking a button on their computer screens. The technology then tabulates the statistical results for you to share with the group during the webinar.

If you are interested in incorporating this type of interaction into your presentation, be sure to ask about the availability of polling upfront, as not all webinar technology providers offer this function. If you aren't going to employ polling in your presentation, don't add it to your consideration scope as you may unnecessarily eliminate some providers from the running. Providers that offer polling include it in their service package; you should not pay extra for it.

Handouts

When presenting your AFW, you often will want to disseminate electronic materials to participants. These materials may be worksheets, white papers, or even a copy of the PowerPoint presentation. Some webinar providers are able to do this for you as part of their registration management services. Add this to your list of "must have" services if you plan to offer handouts and don't have an easy way to distribute them yourself.

Customer Service

Without fail, there will be at least one person who has a technology issue in the webinar. Even if the problem occurs on the participant's end, as it often does, he will still expect help. Therefore, make sure your webinar back-office partner is a gem at customer service. Remember, this is your event, so the customer service that is delivered will reflect upon you, the presenter – regardless of who provides the support. Ask the following when performing due diligence:

- How the provider handles requests for support when attendees encounter technology problems?
- How many customer service representatives do they have on their team to support your webinar?
- How do the attendees access the customer service team?

Also, inquire about how much technical knowledge the customer service department has. They will receive a broad range of questions from "How do I click on a link?" to "How do I install the software?" They must be able to expeditiously handle all questions with the same level of accuracy and professionalism.

Surveys

When the webinar concludes, it is important that you have a means of soliciting attendee feedback through a survey. Most providers include a satisfaction survey as part of their standard package. Review the questions asked on the survey to ensure that you are gathering meaningful information. If not, tailor the questions to your needs. Ideally, you will be able to write your own survey questions; but be aware that some providers charge for this privilege.

The company you select to help you deliver your webinar is a critical step in the development of your AFW webinar program. The technology can support or hinder your ability to provide a high-quality, smoothly running presentation, just as it adds or detracts from the participant experience. After identifying the criteria above that are crucial to you and comparing vendors, request the opportunity to try the platform with some colleagues before making a commitment.

10 Creating an Effective Webinar Presentation

Design PowerPoint® Presentations That Grab and Hold the Attention of Your Virtual Attendees

By Susan Stoen

Now that you know the content you will cover during your attendee-funded webinar (AFW), it is time to create the visual component of your presentation, PowerPoint® slides for PC users and Keynote® slides for Mac users. Creating effective visuals is one of the most important steps in developing an effective skill-based webinar. When you contrast speaking in-person with presenting in a webinar, there is one important difference – your face-to-face connection (or lack thereof) with the audience. When presenting in a webinar environment, you don't have the opportunity to walk the room before the event, greet attendees, set the tone and connect with audience members. With this medium, the primary way you develop rapport with your audience is with your voice and the visuals you show participants during the webinar.

To make up for the lack of face-to-face interaction in webinars, you need to present visuals that demonstrate your professionalism and level of expertise. In fact, these visuals can make or break your credibility and have a significant effect on the attendee experience. This chapter will guide you through simple, yet effective, steps to create a powerful eLearning experience. You will become a more vibrant presenter, and your audience will leave your webinar excited about their skills.

The Presentation Creation Process

The first step in the design of a webinar presentation is determining your key message and supporting content in a slide format. If you have an outline, you can translate your content onto slides. To eliminate this time-consuming step, many speakers instead choose to outline their presentations directly in PowerPoint® or Keynote®.

To engage participants and help them follow your training, create one slide for each thought or idea. In addition to words and phrases, include data, charts, studies, and quotes. To make it easy for attendees to follow along with your presentation – and to ensure that you remember everything you are to deliver – check that the points on your slides match the points outlined in your marketing materials. For example, if your AFW promotions promise that you will teach a five-step process when evaluating job candidates, make sure that your slides list all five steps.

There are many different types of presentations, and not only one model or formula to follow when creating one. There are specific slides that are included in most virtual training presentations. Here is a checklist of those common slides:

- Start with a slide that includes your presentation title, your name, your company name and date of presentation. This is an excellent place to have your photo so the audience can connect a face to the voice.

- Next, present a slide that summarizes the objectives of your training. This also can be thought of as your key message.

- The next slide should present the agenda for the webinar. Show the main topics that you will address throughout your event.

- When presenting a list of points begin with a slide that shows the entire list. Then show separate slides for each individual point. Show these focused slides when you are talking about that particular subtopic. Oftentimes, you may have more than one slide to support these points.

- It is helpful to the audience, and can enhance learning, if you show a slide that recaps your key message (or learning objectives) before you conclude your virtual presentation.

- Conclude your presentation with a slide that shows your contact information. If you want prospects to take the next step, such as visiting your website to download a report or calling for a consultation, mention that offer on this slide, as well. Remember, your attendees paid to be in the webinar so don't be aggressive with your sales pitch. After all, you have their contact information and can follow-up after the session.

Now that your most pertinent content is on slides, you're finished, correct? Wrong! The final step when creating your presentation is to transform all those ideas and thoughts into visual stories for your audience. This is a step that many presenters skip, yet it is as important as gathering the content.

To successfully communicate your message, each presentation needs to include three key elements:

1. **Visual**
2. **Organized**
3. **Memorable**

Presented another way ...

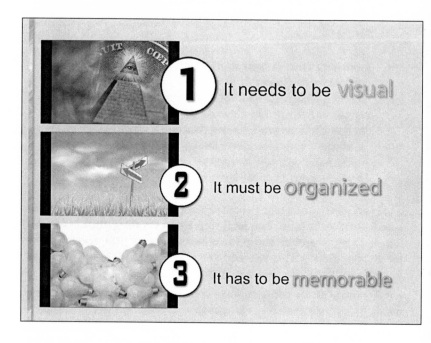

It needs to be visual

It must be organized

It has to be memorable

To successfully communicate your message, your presentation should be visual, organized and memorable.

Element 1: Visual

A visual presentation does not mean slide after slide of bullet points (text). Instead, a visual presentation includes graphical elements, such as diagrams, pictures or charts that communicate with the participants in a completely different way than text-based slides.

Because of the way the human mind processes incoming information (in this case, as a training presentation), it is very important to creatively engage the participant ... visually. Richard E. Mayer, Ph.D., professor of psychology at the University of California, Santa Barbara, has more than 12 years of research in multimedia learning and is the author of *Multimedia Learning*. His research has important implications for PowerPoint® users. In Cliff Atkinson's 2004 article, "The Cognitive Load of PowerPoint® Q&A with Richard E. Mayer," Dr. Mayer addressed this issue with the following response: "Cognitive scientists have discovered three important features of the human information processing system that are particularly relevant for PowerPoint® users: dual-channels, that is, people have separate information processing channels for visual material and verbal material; limited capacity, that is, people can pay attention to only a few pieces of information in each channel at a time; and active processing, that is, people understand the presented material when they pay attention to the relevant material, organize it into a coherent mental structure, and integrate it with their prior knowledge."

The implications of Dr. Mayer's research are:

1. The design of an effective PowerPoint® presentation should leverage both visual and verbal forms.

2. It is easy to overwhelm your audience with slides filled with information that will overload their cognitive systems.

3. The presentations should be designed to help participants select, organize, and integrate the presented information.

So what can you do to make your AFW webinar more visual?

Limit the amount of text on your slides. After you've created your slides, review each one and remove any unnecessary words. Because the purpose of an AFW is to help participants acquire or refine skills, start by eliminating text that does not reinforce the skills being taught. If you believe your audience needs additional information, create handouts that can be distributed to them.

A common reason that slides end up being too text-heavy is that some speakers rely on slides to trigger their memory. One of the perks of presenting in a webinar environment is that the attendees won't see you (unless you use a webcam). Don't make the presentation serve the dual purpose of also being your script. Create whatever notes or outlines you need for your purposes and design the presentation for your audience.

When determining how much text to put on each slide, keep the following guidelines in mind:

- As often as possible, follow the *6 x 6 Rule*, which states: "No slide should have more than six bullet points on it, and no bullet point should contain more than six words."

- In conjunction with the *6 x 6 Rule*, there is another rule that is important to remember: Do not communicate more than one idea per slide. If you find that you have more than one thought or concept on a slide, divide your content between two slides. It won't take you any more time to cover the ideas during your presentation, whether they are on one slide or two. And, you enhance the learning experience for your attendees.

- Consider writing your slide text in headline style, such as newspaper headlines, instead of full sentences. For example, instead of "There are three major ways to increase your company profits," write "3 Ways to Increase Profits."

- Bullet points do not need end punctuation. If you find yourself using periods after your bullet points, you're probably writing full sentences. Take that as an indication that they are too long and rewrite them.

- Eliminate unnecessary adjectives (such as "very" high results or "fabulous" earnings) and articles (words like "and" and "the"). Although these words are acceptable to say as a speaker, they don't belong on your slides.

Don't limit your slide layout to the bullet-point format. Vary the layout from slide to slide. If you review the presentation and find that the majority of your slides use the bullet-point layout, change some slides to other styles.

Test each slide and ask yourself: Is there a way to convey the point visually? Could the information be presented in a table or a graph? What kind of picture or diagram could tell the story? The best way to demonstrate this approach is to show you an example.

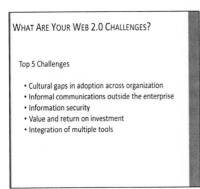

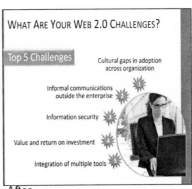

Before   After

Whenever possible, use a picture or diagram to help tell your story.

There are some important considerations when using images in your presentation.

First, make sure the images you are using are not copyright protected. Copying images from the Internet is a poor way to acquire pictures for your presentation because you are likely to violate copyright laws and many Internet images are very low resolution. If you paste low-resolution images onto your slide and resize them, they will look fuzzy (a dead giveaway that you just copied the image from the web). Your credibility is at stake when you are a presenter which means you always want to use high-quality materials - and this suggestion is not limited to webinars. Cheap or poorly designed materials convey a negative impression of your level of knowledge.

The best approach when using images is to create a collection of royalty free stock photos that you can use for your presentations. If you search the web for "royalty-free stock photos" you'll get a number of results that will lead you to sites which offer great images for sale. The starting price is usually around $3 each. Once you purchase them, you can download the photos and use as often as you like in your presentations.

> *For a list of photo websites sites, visit*
> *StopSpeakingForFree.com and enter AFW4ME.*

The same rules apply to images like cartoons. If you want to use cartoons to add humor (a great idea), be sure you're not violating copyright laws. Contact the cartoonist for permission or to acquire the rights to use it.

Element 2: Organized

Your audience will have an easier time understanding and retaining the content you share if it is well-organized. There are a number of ways that presenters can organize their content. Some of these ways are obvious to the audience, while others are more "behind the scenes." But what can you do to make your presentation more organized and easier to follow?

Provide a recurring frame of reference. In other words, provide participants with an agenda. For example, if your webinar contains six major sections, such as an introduction, four agenda topics, and a conclusion, create an agenda slide that lists the major sections of your presentation. Repeat the agenda slide each time you begin a new section of your presentation, so that attendees can follow your road map. By using visual cues to define the structure of your program, you will find it easier to guide participants through the learning process.

Your agenda doesn't have to be a boring, bullet-point list. Get creative with your visuals. Highlight the section you are about to start to make it quickly apparent where you are in the presentation. For example, when you repeat the agenda slide, use animation or a design element (such as a different color font or larger type) to make it clear where you are in your presentation.

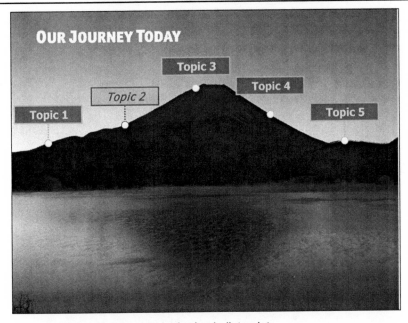

Agenda slides don't have to be boring bullet-points.

Present data in a way that's easy to understand. Create charts and graphs that tell a visual story. You want slides to communicate information at a glance, so participants don't turn their attention away from you to interpret the data you're putting in front of them. If your virtual training requires a lot of detailed spreadsheets or graphs, it's best to create handouts for the participants with that information.

Some graphs are easy to quickly understand while others aren't. The following image is an example of a graph that isn't easy to grasp at first glance. The second image demonstrates how to create a "visual story" to quickly communicate the points you are making.

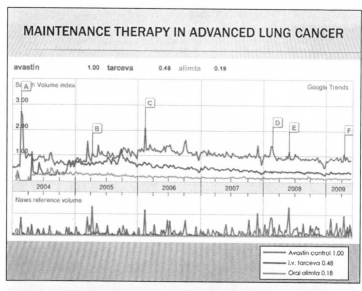

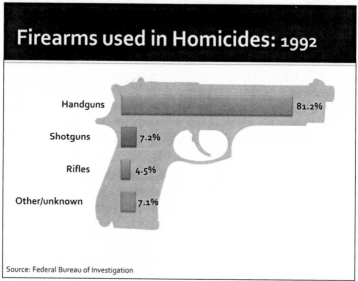

Source: Federal Bureau of Investigation

Use graphics to create "visual stories" that quickly communicate the points you are making in your presentation. The top graphic is ineffective, while the bottom one quickly conveys an effective story.

Help the audience focus on what's important. Similar to your approach with data and graphs, your goal for a visual aid is to never make your audience stop and study to understand the story. The message should be quick and clear. There are some simple techniques to use on your slides that help the audience readily comprehend the point you're trying to make.

- **Use color.** Highlight the concept on which you want the audience to focus. For example, if the text on your slide is primarily black, use red to draw attention to a key statistic or point.

2006 Cancer Deaths - NSW

	Lung	Breast	Prostate	Colorectal	Unknown Primary Site	Pancreas	Non-Hodgkin lymphoma
Number							
Males	1,476	.	968	711	691	361	268
Females	893	933	.	560	668	371	235
Persons	2,369	933	968	1,272	1,359	732	504
Percent							
Males	20.2	.	13.2	9.7	9.4	4.9	3.7
Females	15.4	16.1	.	9.7	11.5	6.4	4.1
Persons	18.1	7.1	7.4	9.7	10.4	5.6	3.8

Use color to draw attention to certain areas of your slides.

> *To view this and other slides in color, visit StopSpeakingForFree.com and enter AFW4ME.*

Use animation. If the webinar technology you're using supports animation (the feature in PowerPoint® that allows you to add motion to a graphical element or text), take advantage of it. Simple movement, such as having an arrow appear that points to a number immediately draws the participants' eyes to that area of the slide. You can also use presenter tools leveraging the webinar technology platform to create motion in your presentation.

Use restraint. When applying animation to any element of your slide, use just enough to capture the attention of the audience, but no more. Crazy spirals or wild flying objects could annoy your viewers, especially in a business environment. They also may not work as well when the presentation is uploaded for webinar delivery because it is delivered via the Internet.

Element 3: Memorable

In addition to your fabulous delivery, there are a number of things you can do to make your presentation more memorable for the audience. Here are some actions you can take to make sure your virtual training event is a memorable experience.

Customize your template. A template is a pattern or blueprint of a slide design. Templates are made up of one or more slide masters. A slide master stores information about the theme and slide layouts of a presentation, including the background, color, fonts, effects, placeholder sizes, and positioning. Every presentation contains at least one slide master, and may contain many different masters. The key benefit to modifying and using slide masters is that you can make universal style changes to every slide in your presentation, including ones added later to the presentation. When you use a slide master, you save time because you don't have to type the same information on more than one slide. The slide master especially comes in handy when you have extremely long presentations with numerous slides. If you want to learn more about templates or slide masters, use your PowerPoint® Help feature. There are a number of articles, videos and training tools that explain them in greater detail.

When presenting a webinar, you have an even greater opportunity (and responsibility) to share top-notch visuals with your audience. What else does your audience have to look at? If your visuals are poorly designed, you can almost guarantee that your audience will be looking at their email during your presentation. In addition to creating visuals that grab and hold your participants' attention, make sure your PowerPoint® template visually reinforces your brand.

Take the time to set up a custom template that includes your logo and utilizes your corporate colors and fonts consistently. There are design firms available for this kind of work.

> Be sure to hire a designer who is familiar with PowerPoint®. If you don't, you may get something that looks nice, but doesn't function well as a template.

Another option is to purchase and download a template from the Internet. If you perform a web search for "PowerPoint® templates," you'll find lots of resources. Many of the templates available for purchase just need your logo added to them, and they'll be ready to use. Avoid using the old "canned" templates that were included with your purchase of PowerPoint®. Purchase or commission a custom template. It will go a long way in making your training more credible and, at the same time, visually reinforce your brand with the audience. If you use the same template that thousands of other presenters have used, how will you set yourself apart? Regardless of what you are doing – from running an ad to mailing a brochure to delivering a webinar – branding is always key.

Use a theme. Remember the visual of a mountain that was used earlier in this chapter as an example of an agenda? In that presentation, the mountain theme was repeated throughout the slides in a number of different ways. The whole presentation revolved around "the journey" and incorporated pictures of people climbing, reaching for, and finally reaching the summit (their goal).

Here are a number of other ideas that can be incorporated into visual themes. You can use these ideas for your template, too.

Theme Idea	Represents
Lighthouse	How your company guides
Bulldog	Tenacity
Chess	Strategy
Puzzle	Problem solving
Toolbox	Solutions
Detective	Finding and providing solutions
Elevator	Go to the next level
Space	New world, new perspective
Running	Achieving goals
Road signs, maps, compass	"How to" and new directions
Rowing	Teamwork, pulling together
Binoculars	Outlook, vision
Maze	Confusion, uncertainty
Stairway, storms	Challenge
Umbrella	Protection
Books, movies, television shows	All great resources for your own theme ideas

Incorporate humor. You don't have to be a stand-up comedian to incorporate humor into the visuals of your training. Adding cartoons or funny pictures to your presentation can be just as effective as telling a joke. The topic of cartoons was addressed earlier in this chapter.

To take your training visuals to the next level, use and apply the techniques presented in this chapter. Also, take notes when you see great visual ideas during training sessions that you attend. By giving your audience visually appealing, organized and memorable slides, you'll help them remain engaged in your presentation. This, in turn, will help them better comprehend and digest your subject matter ... enabling them to leave the session ready to implement their new skills.

About the Author

Susan Stoen is the founder and principal of CQ Communications: The Clarity Quotient. She has been designing and creating clear, compelling business messages for more than 20 years. By combining her passion for communications and design, she has made it her professional mission to identify and bring to her audience the most effective methods to ensure their message is understood, remembered, repeated and acted on. One of her goals is to save audiences everywhere from "Death by PowerPoint®!"

Susan is an energetic and laser-focused consultant, who thrives on unraveling the complex. She is a popular speaker, who addresses topics such as visual communications and the correct way to use PowerPoint® as an effective tool for presenters. Susan can be reached at susan@theclarityquotient.com.

* All graphics in this chapter were created by CQ Communications: The Clarity Quotient. All rights reserved.

Putting It All Together

With all of this information at your finger tips, you are ready to enter the world of attendee-funded webinars (AFWs). Below are the key concepts I hope you learned from reading this book:

1. There is a wonderful opportunity for you to create a new income stream leveraging the power of AFWs.

2. There is a fine-line between free and for-fee webinars of which to be mindful when selecting the topics you will deliver in your AFW.

3. Select topics on which you can clearly demonstrate expertise so you are positioned as a thought leader.

4. *Importance* itself doesn't sell. Position your AFW as both *urgent* and *important* (relevant) to get your prospects to take action on the problem you address.

5. There are three prospect types to leverage: *Fans, Acquaintances,* and *Strangers.* Each group requires a unique marketing approach to generate registrants.

6. With AFWs, you need to be mindful of both buyers and attendees when promoting your events. They aren't always one and the same.

7. Your AFW description creates the perception of your product. Take the time to develop a description that screams to your target market - "This is for you!"

8. Most of your AFW sales will occur within 48 hours of the event so your marketing campaign should be geared to leverage that buying dynamic.

9. Select the right webinar provider to support your virtual training courses based on how you will conduct your session.

10. Be mindful of the nuances of virtual presentations when creating your PowerPoint slides.

To further assist your implementation of the concepts contained in this book, visit StopSpeakingForFree.com and enter the code AFW4ME to access the *Webinar Resource Center* which has:

- Bullet point starters for your webinar description

- AFW Description Creator™ worksheet

- A list of 100 websites that will publish your articles for FREE

- A list of websites on which you can promote your AFW for FREE

- Sample PowerPoint® slides to help you design an effective AFW

- Information on speaking and delivery considerations when delivering a virtual presentation

And much, much more...

About the Authors

Lee B. Salz is the recognized authority on attendee-funded webinars (AFWs). He has successfully guided hundreds of speakers, consultants and trainers into the world of AFWs and *Stop Speaking For Free!*

As a speaker and consultant, Lee recognized the income ceilings that limit the earnings of fellow experts. In response, he launched Business Expert Webinars (BEW), the leader in AFWs , as a way to connect speakers with their target registrants - and get paid! Lee is on a quest to help experts, frustrated by their inability to generate the income they desire, to leverage attendee-funded webinars as a new revenue stream.

The creation of BEW was inspired by Lee's other business venture, Sales Architects, in which he helps companies build scalable, successful sales organizations. In his work with thousands of business professionals, Lee identified a critical factor affecting the profitability of companies - their commitment to enhancing the skills of their employees. He saw that companies could not afford the traditional training approaches due to budget constraints and needed a cost-effective, efficient means to develop the job proficiency of their people. This aligned perfectly with the mission and vision of BEW.

In addition to *Stop Speaking for Free!*, Lee is the author of the award-winning book, *Soar Despite Your Dodo Sales Manager* (WBusinessBooks 2007), which presents his Sales Architecture®

methodology. He is also a columnist for *Sales & Marketing Management* magazine and *SalesforceXP* magazine with a concentration on sales management strategies. He has been quoted in the *Wall Street Journal, New York Times, Dallas Morning News, MSNBC, Selling Power* magazine, *Training* magazine and many other leading media publications.

If you're ready to stop speaking for free, let Lee guide your journey into the world of AFWs. Learn more about Lee Salz and Business Expert Webinars at BusinessExpertWebinars.com.

Jenny L. Hamby is a copywriter and Certified Guerrilla Marketer who specializes in promoting live and virtual training seminars, as well as information products. She works primarily with speakers, trainers, consultants, and coaches who want to create direct-response Internet, advertising and direct-mail campaigns to boost revenue and generate qualified leads for their businesses.

As Business Expert Webinars' marketing expert, Jenny helps speakers create marketing plans to fill their attendee-funded webinars. She has served on the BEW Advisory Board since 2008.

Since 1995, she has marketed a variety of training programs and materials on such diverse topics as financial services, inventory management, negotiations, Neurolinguistic Programming (NLP), trade show marketing, elder and disability law, behavior-based safety, Enterprise Resource Management, and Internet marketing. Her multi-channel marketing campaigns have netted response rates as high as 84 percent … on budgets as small as $125.

Jenny is the creator of "How to Successfully Market Seminars and Workshops," a home-study program that shows professionals how to develop marketing plans and promotional materials to fill seminar seats. To learn how she can help you promote your training events, visit SeminarMarketingPro.com.

LaVergne, TN USA
17 May 2010
182969LV00001B/2/P